HUNTING TERRORISTS IN THE JUNGLE

HUNTING TERRORISTS IN THE JUNGLE

JOHN CHYNOWETH

TEMPUS

In memory of Major Roy Fletcher, 14th/20th King's Hussars, whose hilarious tales of wartime army life enlivened many a long jungle night.

First published 2004
This edition 2007

Tempus Publishing Limited
The Mill, Brimscombe Port,
Stroud, Gloucestershire, GL5 2QG
www.tempus-publishing.com

British Library Cataloguing in Publication Data.
A catalogue record for this book is available from the British Library.

ISBN 978 0 7524 4315 7

Typesetting and origination by Tempus Publishing Limited
Printed and bound in Great Britain

Contents

FOREWORD

By General Tun Ibrahim bin Ismail, Chief of the Malaysian Armed Forces Staff, 1970–77.

I was delighted to be asked by my friend John Chynoweth to write a short foreword for *Hunting Terrorists in the Jungle.* The book gives an account of his personal experiences while serving as a British National Service officer seconded to serve in the Malay Regiment, fighting the communist terrorists at the height of the Malayan Emergency. He has based his account on the letters he wrote to his parents during the time he was serving in the 6th Battalion in 1953 and 1954. During this time we became close comrades-in-arms, and developed a friendship which has lasted for over fifty years.

I am sure that readers will find the book interesting, not only to read about the conditions of the people and the country at the time of the Emergency, but also because it expresses the views and experiences of a very young officer who was drafted straight after completing his university education in the United Kingdom, to fight the communist terrorists in the steaming jungles of Malaya.

Ibrahim bin Ismail
Kuala Lumpur
May 2004

List of Maps and Diagrams

Glossary of Military Abbreviations and Malay Words

Military Abbreviations

ADC	Aide-de-Camp
C-in-C	Commander in Chief
CO	Commanding Officer
CQMS	Company Quarter Master Sergeant
CSM	Company Sergeant Major
DFC	Distinguished Flying Cross
DSO	Distinguished Service Order
GHQ	General Headquarters
GOC	General Officer Commanding
HMT	Her Majesty's Transport
HQ	Headquarters
INA	Indian National Army
IRA	Irish Republican Army
MC	Military Cross
MM	Military Medal
NCO	Non-commissioned officer
OBE	Order of the British Empire
OC	Officer Commanding
RASC	Royal Army Service Corps
REME	Royal Electrical and Mechanical Engineers
RFC	Royal Flying Corps
RN	Royal Navy
RSM	Regimental Sergeant Major
STS	Special Training School
TA	Territorial Army
VC	Victoria Cross
WOSB	War Office Selection Board
WRAC	Women's Royal Army Corps

MALAY WORDS

The spellings are taken from the *Dictionary of Colloquial Malay* by R. Winstedt (Singapore, 1957). Some have subsequently changed.

Atap	Palm thatch
Belukar	Secondary jungle
Imam	Muslim priest
Joget	A Malay dance
Kampong	Malay village
Ladang	Clearing or plantation
Lalang	Tall coarse grass
Orang Asli	Native man = Aborigine = Sakai
Padang	An open field
Parang	Heavy jungle knife
Rongging	A Malay dance
Sakai	Aborigine
Sungai	River
Tenku	Prince
Tuan	Sir
Tun	Lord

Preface

In 1948 some 5,000 armed Malayan Chinese communists began an insurgency aimed at overthrowing the British colonial government of Malaya.[1] During the next twelve years thousands of National Servicemen who had been conscripted into the British Army were sent to operate in the jungle against these terrorists. A few National Service subalterns (of which I and two others were the first three) were seconded from their British infantry regiments to join the Malay Regiment, which in 1953 was still mainly officered by the British, though the number of Malay officers was steadily increasing.[2] Because the London insurance market would not cover Malayan businesses against losses incurred during a civil war, the authorities called the conflict an 'Emergency', not a war.

Chapter 1 describes the reasons why National Service was introduced, the deployment of the conscripts and my experiences while being trained as a recruit and as an officer cadet. Chapter 2 describes Malaya as it was in the 1950s, gives a brief history of British involvement in the country, outlines the origins of the Emergency and summarises the events of the first five years of the conflict. Chapters 3, 4 and 5 detail my experiences during jungle operations in 1953 and 1954, as recorded in sixty-eight letters which I wrote home at the time. The extracts from these letters are supplemented by notes explaining some of the contents, by information subsequently acquired, and by descriptions of incidents deliberately not mentioned in the letters. Chapter 6 contains my views of the errors committed by the Army High Command from 1948 until 1954, and Chapter 7 describes the final years of the Emergency and provides an assessment of the communist leader Chin Peng. An Epilogue describes the aftermath of my experiences. No concessions to political correctness have been made, partly because the book describes life before this particular affectation became widespread, but mainly because I believe that it is more important to use accurate words than to try to appease certain minorities by using inappropriate or misleading terms.

The book is intended to interest National Servicemen, those who served in the Army in Malaya during the Emergency, those of the younger

British generations who know little about either subject and Malaysian citizens who would like to read about the defeat of that communist insurrection. Two events prompted me to write this book. Going through some old family papers in 2003 I came across the letters I had written home from Malaya fifty years earlier. My parents had insisted that as their only child I should write home regularly, and though I wanted to keep a diary I found that I did not have the time or energy to do both. There were, of course, significant differences between the contents of the letters and the entries I would have made in a diary. To prevent my parents becoming concerned the former usually omitted incidents which might have put me at risk while the latter would have contained more complete descriptions of my thoughts, feelings, actions and experiences. As an historical record, a diary would have been more valuable than the letters, although I did make the letters as detailed as possible and the editorial notes now added fill in some of the gaps. In November 1914, Captain Harry Dillon, an infantry officer, wrote home from Ypres, 'I am glad you have kept my letters as it is impossible to keep a diary, and if alive I should like to look through them later and write up the gaps'. Not all First World War officers opted for letters instead of diaries. Captain Harry Yoxall, another infantry officer on the Western Front, both wrote letters and kept a diary which he stated was a more faithful record of his thoughts and activities since in his letters he constantly had to reassure his family that he was not taking unnecessary risks. As he was awarded an MC and bar he certainly took risks, whether unnecessary or not.[3]

Reading my letters again for the first time in fifty years I was surprised by the amount of information about the Emergency they contained, and I began to make extracts as I thought that the Imperial War Museum might like to have a copy for their archives.

The second event which prompted me to write this book was the decision of the seventy-nine-year-old Chin Peng, the Malayan Chinese leader of the communist terrorists during the Emergency, to publish in October 2003 his version of events; this has enabled me to write a book which incorporates both his views and mine. Few books about war tell the story from both sides' points of view because usually the authors only have access to their own side's sources of information. There was, of course, a huge disparity between the relative importance of the two authors at the time of these events. Chin Peng was, for the twelve years of the Emergency, the leader of a terrorist army which at peak numbered about 10,000 men, and was responsible for all his side's military and political decisions. As a National Service subaltern in the Malay Regiment I commanded forty soldiers for just over a year, and spent my time trekking through the jungle with my platoon laying ambushes, destroying food dumps and cultivations and searching for enemy camps. I played no part, of course, in military or political decision-making, though I developed strong views about certain policies of our High Command. A critique of Chin Peng's book is given in Chapter 7, but I have quoted some of his more interesting statements whenever I think there is a reasonable chance that they may be accurate.

Looking back at my two years of National Service I recognise that it had a greater effect on me than any similar length of time before or since. It involved exposure to completely new lifestyles, to people of different social backgrounds, races and colour, to colleagues of widely different characters and abilities, to tropical climes and wildlife, to physically challenging tasks and unexpected medical problems, to hilarious moments and frightening incidents, and to the responsibility for commanding men. Although as a National Service subaltern I received only half the pay of a regular subaltern while doing the same work and running the same risks, I thoroughly enjoyed my two years, and am deeply grateful for having had the opportunity to serve in the Army.

I would like to record my thanks to the following friends who helped me with this book: General Tun Ibrahim bin Ismail (who served with me in B Company, 6th Battalion, the Malay Regiment when he was a captain) for writing the foreword; Simon Pritchard (The Queen's Own Royal West Kents) and Tony Froom (The Buffs), who served with me as subalterns in the 6th Battalion, for correcting some factual errors in my early drafts, for supplying additional information and for discussing with me our differing memories of certain shared experiences; to Janet Lewis, late of Lady Margaret Hall, Oxford, Colonel Hugh Boscawen (The Coldstream Guards), Lieutenant Commander Brian Toomey, RN (Retd) and Major Nigel Magrane (The Royal Irish Rangers, Retd), who all provided detailed and helpful comments on my later drafts.

In 1953, at the age of sixty-three, Duff Cooper wrote an autobiography entitled *Old Men Forget*, and while this title is unfortunately only too true, I hope my readers will accept that most of my book is based on the letters which I wrote home as a young man at the time of the events I describe. Cooper, however, had a worrying comment about the inaccuracy of later memories of wartime experiences. After the First World War he enjoyed telling the story of what happened one night in France in 1918 when, as a subaltern, he was leading a patrol which got lost in No-Man's Land. He looked up at the stars, and his knowledge of astronomy told him that they were heading straight for the German trenches, and his immediate about-turn saved their lives. He was always convinced of the truth of this tale until years later when he looked up the appropriate entry in the diary he had kept at the time, and found no mention of the event.[4] Most incidents involving personal danger were omitted from my letters home for obvious reasons, but I have tried hard not to embellish my later descriptions with what Duff Cooper called false memories of wartime feats, or with what some more recent writers have called 'sexing-up'.

John Chynoweth
Taunton
Somerset
January 2007

Notes (See the Bibliography for the full references of endnotes)

1 'Malayan Chinese' were Chinese people who lived in Malaya. The Malays are a distinct race.
2 When Malaya became independent in 1957, the Malay Regiment was renamed the Royal Malay Regiment, or Askar Melayu Di-Raja in Malay.
3 Brown, p.31.
4 Cooper, pp.81-2.

CHAPTER 1

NATIONAL SERVICE

Note: In 1953, Malaysia, Thailand and Sri Lanka were called Malaya, Siam and Ceylon respectively, and the earlier names have been retained in this book because they were those in use at the time. The names of some Army colleagues have been changed to preserve their privacy.

On 26 July 1945 a Labour Government was elected in Britain with a big majority, partly due to the large number of postal votes their candidates had received from members of the armed forces. Three weeks later, following the dropping of two atomic bombs, Japan surrendered, thus ending the Second World War. The new Labour Government hastened to meet the wishes of the wartime conscripts by demobilising them as soon as possible, and this soon left only a small regular Army, Navy and Air Force to fulfil our continuing military commitments. These involved preparing to defend our country from a possible attack by the Soviet Union while maintaining peace in our colonies during the planned contraction of our Empire, which was to be achieved by granting independence to those colonies considered ready to receive it. Within a few years these commitments increased greatly as the Cold War developed, as terrorism escalated in Aden, Cyprus, Kenya, Malaya, Northern Ireland, Palestine and elsewhere, and war began in Korea. The regular forces had insufficient manpower to cope with all these problems, so in 1947 the Labour Government, supported by the Conservative Opposition, introduced National Service which continued until 1963. The measure was opposed by some seventy Labour MPs and by all the Liberal MPs.

The legislation required all fit males aged between eighteen and twenty-six to join one or other of the three armed services for eighteen months, a period which in 1950 was extended to two years. Students undertaking further education could delay joining up until they had completed their studies. Because of shortages of labour, coal miners, merchant seamen, fishermen, farm workers and policemen were exempt. One in ten of those liable for National Service were chosen by ballot to become coal miners. These were called 'Bevin boys', after the wartime Minister of Labour who had first introduced this measure. After demobilisation, conscripts had to spend three and a half years in the reserves. During the sixteen years of National Service more than one million men were conscripted into the Army.[1]

Though in 1947 Britain was supposedly at peace with the world, it was not long before our young men were fighting African, Arab, Cypriot, Irish, Jewish and Malayan Chinese terrorists in various countries, and North Korean and Chinese armies in Korea, so the conscripts could be forgiven for wondering quite what the words 'universal peace' and 'United Nations' actually meant. In addition, National Servicemen were involved in operations in aid of the civil powers in Bahrain, Barbados, Belize, British Guiana, Cameroun, the Gold Coast, Guatemala, Hong Kong, Jamaica, Jordan, Kuwait, Singapore, Somali Republic, Togo, and Zanzibar.[2]

By 1952 the concept of National Service was opposed by more than half the British public, and was unpopular with most conscripts when they were called up.[3] Low pay, primitive accommodation, bullying NCOs, separation from family and friends, interruption of careers and boring or dangerous postings compared unfavourably with the comforts of home life and the rewards of civilian occupations. After they had completed their service, however, many felt that they had benefited from the experience. Those in the regular Army were not entirely happy with National Service either, because the training of thousands of conscripts a year required many regular officers and NCOs and this, of course, substantially reduced the number of experienced men available for deployment on active service. Some regulars considered that National Service was not cost-effective because of the relatively short time the conscripts had to serve after completing their training, and some were also uncertain about the motivation of the recruits. They believed that young men who had been called up in 1940 to oppose a seemingly imminent German invasion of England would have served with more dedication than those called up in 1950 to risk their lives chasing terrorists in some distant colony. The location of many of our smaller colonies was unknown to most National Servicemen, who had no idea of what was going on there, or why they were being forced to do something about it. The performance on active service of British infantry regiments largely manned by National Servicemen, however, suggests that most of the doubts about their motivation were misplaced.

Young men intending to go to university had to decide whether to go there straight from school while deferring their call-up for three years, or do their National Service straight from school and go to university after being demobilised two years later. Both options had pros and cons. I chose the first, and deferred my National Service until I had taken a degree at the London School of Economics. On 7 August 1952, aged twenty-one, I arrived at Buller Barracks in Aldershot to begin eight weeks of basic training in the Royal Army Service Corps (now part of the Royal Logistic Corps).

Many units in the Army had nicknames based on the initial letters of their titles, and the RASC had over the years acquired several derogatory names. Initially called the Land Transport Corps (nickname, 'London Thieving Corps') the title was changed to the Military Train (nickname, 'Murdering Thieves') which was later changed to the Army Service Corps (nickname, 'Ally Sloper's Cavalry' after a buffoon of that name in a Victorian comic strip cartoon).[4] This was not the only corps to have derogatory nicknames. During the First World War some stretcher bearers were accused of stealing valuables from dead or wounded soldiers, so the initials of the Royal Army Medical Corps were held to stand for 'Rob All My Comrades'.[5] The Intelligence Corps' cap badge of a flower above sprays of laurel leaves was said to represent a pansy resting on its laurels.[6]

I was unhappy at having been called up into a unit which was clearly not well regarded by many in the Army, and I believed that I had been posted there because my degree in economics meant that I was destined to be employed on something boring like the supervision of military stores. Accordingly I determined to transfer to the infantry as soon as possible, although I was told I would not be allowed to do so until I had completed my basic training.

My time at Buller Barracks was an uncomfortable experience accompanied, fortunately, by a steep learning curve. The barracks had been built in the 1890s and were named after General Sir Redvers Buller, who in Victorian times had been admired for his VC and criticised for his military blunders during the Boer War. In the 1930s it had reputedly been condemned as being unfit for human habitation, but twenty years later it was thought to be quite suitable for National Servicemen. As soon as National Service ended it was, of course, immediately rebuilt for use by regulars.[7] Fortunately, I was not there in the winter when, reportedly, no heating was available, but even in summer the lack of any hot water, and the queues for wash basins which had no plugs, contrasted adversely with home facilities for personal hygiene.

Most of my problems during basic training arose from not being an impressive military figure, with glasses (I was very short-sighted) and my ignorance of everything to do with soldiering. Although my father had been an infantry officer in Ireland, France and Italy from 1916 to 1919, he had told me little about his experiences, and I had received no military training at school or university. Basic training at Buller Barracks consisted of lessons in drill, weapons and shooting. Our sergeant was unhelpful. When our kit was tossed at us over the counter of the quartermaster's stores on the first day I did not realise that I had been mistakenly given two left-hand webbing straps instead of one left-hand and one right-hand strap. Having tried and failed to attach them to my pack I approached the sergeant. 'I wonder whether you would be kind enough to help me, sergeant?' I asked politely.

'F**k off,' was the reply. Whenever I had had a problem at home, at school, or at university, any request for help had always resulted in willing assistance, so this response was a little surprising. Had I known at the time what one author had written about basic training I would have been better prepared for Day 2. He wrote: 'In almost every squad there was one victim who had to be picked on [by the NCOs] – the bespectacled grammar school boy with the polite accent …'[8]

That was an accurate description of me. When we appeared on the parade ground for the first time, I did not know that a newly issued army beret should have been soaked in water overnight in order to persuade it when worn to stay drooped smartly over one ear. My beret stood tall like a chef's hat. The previous owner of the belt I had been issued with must have weighed 15 stone compared with my 10 stone, as it was so long that it dangled down below my waist because I did not know how to shorten it. The long laces of my army boots were a problem, which I solved by tying double bow knots, but the army solution of course was different – wind twice round the ankles and tie with reef knots. When the drill sergeant arrived in front of me on the square, he eyed me up and down with contempt. 'What the f**k have we got here?' he demanded, knocking my upstanding beret off my head with his drill stick, 'a f***ing cook?' He next grasped my dangling belt and bounced me up and down. 'No', he said, 'a f***ing cowboy!' He then spotted the smart bows on my boots and turned puce. 'Twice round the parade ground at the f***ing double,' he bellowed. The use of foul language was widespread, and words starting with 'f' were included in almost everything said by the NCOs.

In spite of apparently being an ideal candidate for bullying, it did not last long as I learned quickly, and being three years older than most recruits I was better able to stand up for myself. I soon found that tipping junior NCOs solved many difficulties. Half a crown (12½p) to a lance corporal produced a smart pack boxed out with hardboard. Five shillings (25p) to the same man hired a soldering iron to burn off the dimples on the leather of the toe caps of my new army boots and enabled the resulting smooth finish to be polished to an excellent shine. A ten shilling note (50p) to a corporal in the arms store retrieved my rifle which had been taken into custody for being left unattended under my bed during my first weekend leave. I later discovered that this corporal spent his weekends searching the barracks for unattended rifles, which he locked away in the arms store until their owners arrived on Monday mornings to hear that they would be court-martialled unless they paid to receive back their weapon.

My fellow recruits provided some memorable moments. A solicitor who occupied a bed next to mine told me on our first day in the barracks that he was going to get out of the Army as soon as possible in order to get on with his career. He had a mild dose of athlete's foot, and sat up in bed for the whole of the first night scratching his feet. In the morning they were two raw and bloody stumps, and he hobbled off to report sick. We never saw him again. At the time I was furious that he had escaped two years' conscription through a medical fraud, but on reflection I decided that with his attitude he would have been useless as a soldier anyway. One evening a corporal came into our barrack room carrying a wooden toilet seat and a roll of wire wool. 'Princess … is visiting the orficers' mess for lunch tomorrow,' he announced with a smirk. 'This 'ere is the seat she will sit on in the bog, and it's got to be smoothed by you lot. I'll collect it tomorrow morning, and if it ain't like glass you'll all be on a charge.' We took it in turns to work on it with wire wool and wax polish, and the seat duly passed muster the following day, but if Her Royal Highness had heard the remarks which accompanied its handling she would have squirmed with embarrassment. Supplying suitable toilet seats for royal use was apparently not an unusual problem for military hosts. During the wartime North African campaign, General Montgomery's ADC was ordered to find a seat for the thunderbox of the visiting King George VI, and told to find one that had not been freshly painted.[9]

Towards the end of basic training I was put into a squad named POCs (Potential Officer Cadets), which was pronounced 'Pox' and called 'Potential Officer C**ts' by the other conscripts. To obtain a commission it was necessary first to pass the War Office Selection Board (WOSB) which was held at Warminster. This was a daunting experience, not helped by the lies and rumours one heard before attending. The obstacle course was impossible to complete, the tests of initiative were so difficult that everyone failed, table manners were monitored and reported on by spies, the compulsory five-minute lecturettes were ridiculed by criticism and the final interview would be humiliating. None of these things turned out to be true, though the three days at Warminster were quite testing. A friend failed through bad luck. When he knocked on the door of the office of the major who was conducting the final interviews, and was told to come in, he opened the door with difficulty because it appeared to be jammed. When he finally forced his way in he was set upon by an alsatian which had been lying behind the door. Showing officer-like qualities of courage and initiative he kicked it away, but the major who owned the dog was furious, and put in an adverse report. The Army thus lost a first-class potential young officer, and retained a stupid block head. No more than 70 per cent of candidates passed any WOSB, but some who failed were allowed to re-apply a few months later.

After passing, I applied to transfer to the infantry, and was briefed by a friendly young officer in Aldershot about the RASC Colonel who would interview me about my request. When the Colonel heard that I wanted to leave the corps in order to see some action, he pointed to his missing left ear and asked how I thought he had lost it. Thanks to my informant I was able to remind him that it had been lost when he had overturned his jeep in a ditch after a mess night. 'Get out!' he shouted, which is my last memory of Buller Barracks.

I was surprised to have been accepted into the infantry because I was so short-sighted that, had I lost my glasses during combat, I would have been absolutely useless as a platoon commander. However, in those days this did not seem to be a problem for the Army. I was told that despite my glasses I could apply to be commissioned into any regiment I liked, though my grammar school education and lack of a private income would, of course, rule out the Guards and the Cavalry. We trained at Eaton Hall Officer Cadet School near Chester, the estate of which was owned by the Duke of Westminster, and some cadets were accommodated in comfortable rooms in the Hall, but most (including me) slept in Nissen huts in the grounds.

I arrived at Eaton Hall in October 1952, and my intake of around fifty-four officer cadets was divided into two squads, each with a regular captain in charge. Our captain was an extremely keen man who had played soccer for the Army and was due to join his regiment in Korea at the end of our course. He was determined to maintain his fitness and thus drove us hard, so while the other squad returned from exercises by lorry, we were doubled back to camp. The course lasted sixteen weeks, which was the same length of time as the officer cadet courses in 1917,[10] but in the early 1950s regular army officer cadets trained at Sandhurst for eighteen months.

Physical training was a major part of our programme with route marches, assault courses, and exercises on the moors of North Wales. Digging trenches that winter in frozen ground made me appreciate the efforts of our soldiers in France during the First World War. Lectures were delivered on various topics, though fatigue and the boring subject matter (such as Hygiene or Military Law) meant that many cadets dozed off.

On one of our moorland exercises one of my squad lost his bayonet, but instead of bribing an NCO in the stores to supply a replacement, he took possession of another cadet's weapon. Thus began a long saga of twenty-seven cadets all trying to retain or lay hands on twenty-six bayonets. Everyone except the unlucky one slept with his bayonet under his pillow. Practical jokes soon began. On the parade ground one day I was standing to attention in the front rank when someone in the rank behind whispered, 'Where's your bayonet, John?' Although I was certain it had been on my belt when I had arrived on parade I instinctively lifted my left hand to check that it was still there (it was, of course). My movement was spotted by the major who was taking the parade, and he told the drill sergeant to double me off to the guardroom. I was duly charged with idleness on parade and sentenced to five nights standing behind the stables in Field Service Marching Order, and being subjected to inspection for minute failings in the perfection of my polished boots and numerous brasses. The repercussions of the major's action are described in the notes to my letter of 22 October 1953 in Chapter 4.

There were one or two sad incidents. From time to time we had to spend a night on guard duty, patrolling the grounds and Hall in case of attack by the IRA. This duty was highly unpopular as we were usually tired out after the day's work. Each cadet had to patrol for two hours and then return to the guardroom for a break, before beginning another patrol. One cadet, the son of a serving Colonel, sat down for a rest while on patrol, fell asleep, was caught by the orderly officer and put on a train back to his unit the following morning. His next meeting with his father must have been a nightmare. Because of his arrest I was ordered to take his place on patrol, and while wandering through the library in the Hall I stupidly thought a brief sit down would be quite safe as, in view of what had happened to my unlucky colleague, I was determined to stay awake. Fortunately my chin hit my chest and woke me up just before the orderly officer entered the library otherwise I would have been on the morning train as well. During the First World War falling asleep on sentry duty was an offence for which the maximum punishment, if found guilty by court-martial, was execution by firing squad, though all except two such sentences were commuted to terms of imprisonment. Keeping awake while exhausted is very difficult, and on the Western Front some sleepy sentries held the tips of the bayonets on their rifles under their chins so that if their heads dropped they would wake immediately.[11]

Training culminated at a camp at Okehampton in Devon where we spent three days on Dartmoor fighting mock battles. On the first day I sprained both ankles by stepping into rabbit holes while running through heather, which made the double back to camp at the end of each day extremely painful, but fear of being put back to the beginning of the course if I reported sick meant I had to grin and bear it.

The officer cadets varied widely in their backgrounds and regimental destinations. Some public schoolboys from wealthy families would join the Guards and spend time at Buckingham Palace, while one Jewish cadet of foreign extraction was commissioned into the Pioneer Corps to reputedly supervise the digging of latrines on the moors. Most joined county regiments with which they had family or locational connections. A few had unusual backgrounds. In my squad was an ex-RAF bomber pilot called Stan Balding who during the war had been decorated with a DFC. Discharged in 1945, he had tried a variety of civilian jobs (including selling vacuum cleaners door-to-door) and had finally decided to get back into the forces. Rejected by the RAF on medical grounds (he had been severely burned in a crash landing), he was accepted into the REME. One evening at Eaton Hall, Stan was walking across the parade ground when a staff car containing a major-general stopped to enquire the way to the officers' mess. After receiving directions, the general said: 'Bit old to be a cadet aren't you?' Stan bent down so that his Flying Officer Kite moustache filled much of the open window. 'Asking for a poke in the earhole?' he enquired, before striding off. Fortunately, the general, no doubt impressed by the ribbon of the DFC, laughed, and told his driver to go on.

My closest friend in the squad, Alan Bevans, was slim, dark-haired, good looking, and to my great envy, irresistible to women. One evening we were watching a horror film in a cinema in Chester when a particularly unexpected and startling scene caused many of the audience to rise out of their seats. When matters calmed down, Alan found he was holding the hand of a young lady who was sitting next to him. He whispered something in her ear, raised his eyebrows at me, and they left the cinema. He tottered back to camp at dawn the following morning just in time to change for a route march, towards the end of which he had to be helped along by his friends. His attraction for women eventually proved fatal for his military career. When he joined his regiment, which was then based in the West Indies, he soon acquired two local mistresses, one black and one white. One evening both arrived in camp to visit him, and when the black girl found him embracing the white girl the two young ladies began to fight outside his billet. Unfortunately for Alan, his commanding officer happened to be passing by, and stopped to ask what the bloody hell was going on. Alan was sent to the jungles of Belize for the rest of his tour, and his short service commission was not converted into a regular commission as he had hoped.

When towards the end of the course we were asked to nominate the regiments into which we wished to be commissioned, I chose a county regiment with a distinguished history. I was pleased that they accepted me, but I was disappointed to discover that, because they then had a full complement of subalterns (so I was told) I had to be seconded to some colonial regiment for the remainder of my service. I had recently seen a film in Chester about Beau Geste of the Foreign Legion, and had been impressed by the appearance of a band of Tureg tribesmen brandishing swords while riding camels on their way to attack his desert fort, so when I was asked to nominate an overseas regiment to which I would like to be seconded I chose the camel-riding Somaliland Scouts. A fellow cadet asked to be seconded to the Malay Regiment because he had been born in Malaya, spoke fluent Malay and had parents who lived there. Anyone with experience of the Army will know exactly what happened next. I was posted to the Malay Regiment and he was posted to the Somaliland Scouts.

Other cadets had similar experiences. The actor David Niven, who was at Sandhurst in 1928, had family connections with the Argyll & Sutherland Highlanders, whose Colonel told him that all he had to do in order to be commissioned into the regiment (which was about to be sent to Bermuda which was then regarded as the perfect overseas posting) was to pass his final exams. Niven duly passed, but made a disastrous mistake when filling in the War Office form on which he had to name, in order of preference, three regiments into which he wished to be commissioned. He wrote:

1 The Argyll & Sutherland Highlanders
2 The Black Watch
3 Anything but the Highland Light Infantry

All who have been in the Army will know the outcome – he was commissioned into the Highland Light Infantry and posted to Malta, which was a far less attractive location than Bermuda. As he ruefully admitted: 'Somebody at the War Office was funnier than I was'.[12]

Like most young Englishmen at the time, all I knew about Malaya was that it was somewhere in the Far East, and was having a little local difficulty with terrorists. A glance at an atlas showed that it was a peninsular stretching down from Siam to the island of Singapore, but it took a lot longer to learn much about the communist insurgency that had begun there five years earlier. I did, however, find a book about the history of the regiment I would shortly be joining.

In 1933 the nucleus of an experimental company was recruited at Port Dickson depot on the west coast of Malaya, with twenty-five men chosen from more than 1,000 ethnic Malay applicants. The company was successful, and by 1935 the regiment was nearly 500 strong. The soldiers were initially led by British officers, the first four Malay officers being commissioned in 1936. By the time the Japanese invaded in December 1941, the regiment had two battalions, both of which fought well against the invaders. As soon as the Japanese surrendered in 1945, many regimental survivors reported for duty, and the post-war resurrection of the regiment began. By the time I arrived in 1953 the regiment had six battalions, each being known by its number, i.e. 1 Malay, 2 Malay, and so on.[13]

After leaving Eaton Hall and enjoying my embarkation leave, I was ordered to report to my English regiment's depot to spend a week there before joining a troopship at Liverpool to sail to Singapore. I never understood the reason for this order, but I duly reported to the adjutant, asked him what he would like me to do in the coming week, and was told 'Nothing'. I then went to the officers' mess where my 'Good morning, gentlemen' was ignored by the half dozen or so majors and captains who were sitting around with the newspapers, and not one of them spoke to me while I stood drinking a cup of coffee. Furious at this reception, I left the depot immediately and enjoyed another week's leave before going to Liverpool. The repercussions of this event are described in the Epilogue.

At Liverpool I boarded HMT *Empire Halladale*, an elderly ship built in Hamburg in 1922. She carried an infantry battalion en route to Korea together with a number of posted officers like myself who had no responsibility for the troops on board, and a few nurses, service women, and army officers' wives.[14] The ditty 'Slightly slower than a snail sailed *The Empire Halladale*' which circulated on board explained the six weeks it took us to reach Singapore instead of the four weeks it took most other troopships.

I was pleased to find I would share a cabin with Simon Pritchard who had been at Eaton Hall with me and who was also seconded to the Malay Regiment. I had a batman who cleaned my kit, and a girl in the Women's Royal Army Corps who did my washing and ironing in return for packets of cigarettes. Soon after boarding I was approached by a not-very-young lieutenant in the Royal Army Pay Corps who invited me to join his poker school. I replied that I played bridge but not poker, that I could not afford to lose money at cards, and that my father had warned me about fellows like him. He protested that his poker school was for beginners, and that I would lose trifling amounts until we got to Suez, and would win thereafter. I agreed to give it a trial, and it proved to be highly entertaining. Simon joined too and it filled our days, starting after breakfast in the lounge and finishing in a cabin late at night. Although our tutor had survived more than one court of enquiry into his financial conduct (which is presumably why he was not a captain), he was entirely honest in his dealings with us.

There were about 1,500 men on board, but only a couple of dozen women, so nobody below the rank of major had any chance of a romantic interlude. Before the war the *Halladale* had reputedly been one of Hitler's 'Strength through Joy' liners, on whose cruises many young male and female Nazis had done whatever was necessary to increase the size of Germany's population. This historical background seemed to have affected one army wife who made herself available to senior officers, and when we reached the warmer climes she was often spotted on the upper deck at night with a male companion engaged in the popular pre-war activity. Her behaviour confirmed the truth of another ditty which circulated on board, namely, 'When the weather gets sultry, you gets your adultery.'

The only memory I have of our passage through the Suez Canal is of seeing an Arab squatting on the east bank with his robe hitched up to his waist exposing his genitals to the gaze of those of us who happened to be looking over the ship's rail at the scenery. He was masturbating, presumably to show his contempt for the British who had military bases nearby and whose presence in Egypt was disliked by the natives. The shouted advice he received from the watching soldiers is, unfortunately, unprintable.

Shortly after the ship left Colombo, one of the soldiers on board developed religious mania, made his way up to the bridge, and ordered the

Captain to steer for Jerusalem. He was clapped into a dungeon below the waterline, but was allowed out to exercise on deck for half an hour each evening. On his second evening out he jumped overboard, and pandemonium ensued. It takes a long time to turn a 14,000-ton ship round, and the Indian Ocean contains sharks. The crew raced to the lifeboats, and the 1,500 troops raced to the rails on the starboard side to watch the rescue. The combined weight of the men must have been over 100 tons, and from the orders to disperse yelled over the tannoy by the Captain, it appeared that he thought we might capsize. The lifeboat scene was a disgrace. When the covers were taken off some of the boats they were found to be full of rainwater, while others were missing their drainage plugs. When the first boat was lowered it swung into the side of the ship and smashed an oar. Once in the water, the boats drifted round in circles. By this time more than an hour had gone by and the crazed soldier had swum back to the ship, and was holding on to the rudder. There were many red faces among the crew who encountered much jeering from the troops. The Captain was furious, and ordered endless lifeboat drills from then on. Our poker school was badly disrupted as every time these drills took place we had to evacuate the lounge and stand around for ages doing nothing. I don't know how many other soldiers have jumped overboard from troopships, but a Canadian soldier who had become mentally disturbed by the fear of being torpedoed did so in 1915 while crossing from Quebec to Plymouth. The troopship (the *Carpathia*, which had rescued the surviving passengers from the *Titanic*) stopped, but rough weather prevented the lowering of a boat so the soldier drowned.[15]

I was orderly officer on one occasion in the Indian Ocean and did not find it an enjoyable experience. Accompanied by a warrant officer I visited the soldiers' mess at lunchtime and asked the obligatory question: 'Any complaints?' Instead of the mandatory: 'No, Sir!' that I had been told at Eaton Hall to expect, I was bombarded with complaints shouted from all quarters of the mess. I listened for some time, announced that I would take them up with the appropriate authorities, and departed. When I reported this to the ship's adjutant, I was told that there were no appropriate authorities. That night, before 'Lights Out', I had to inspect the troopdeck which was below the waterline. The warrant officer preceded me, called the men to attention, and I then fell down the ladder and landed in a heap at the bottom (I'd had a few drinks after dinner). What an impressive arrival! The warrant officer looked around the deck and said to the nearest soldier: 'What's the matter with that firehose?' pointing to a coil of hose on a bulkhead. The man said he didn't know, and nor did I, so when the warrant officer said: 'The orderly officer has also spotted the fault', I thought he was about to ask me to describe it to the men, so I said, 'That's enough', and climbed back up the ladder. The soldiers' sleeping accommodation was appalling – hammocks slung on unventilated decks in tropical temperatures. Many chose to sleep up on the open decks, hard on the body though they were.

When we docked at Singapore, Simon and I were met by Richard Birchenough, a very friendly major in the Malay Regiment, who took us in his Jaguar to a hotel for lunch, and then to the Singapore Swimming Club for the afternoon. He answered dozens of questions before taking us to the railway station to board the night train to cross the causeway into Malaya.

Notes

1 Royle, pp.22, 25.
2 Ibid., p.201.
3 Ibid., p.199.
4 Carew, pp.124-25.
5 van Emden, pp.87-88.
6 Gaylor, p.103.
7 Sutton, p.729.
8 Royle, p.41.
9 *The Daily Telegraph*, 20 December 2003, p.23, obituary of Johnny Henderson.
10 Cooper, p.67.
11 Putkowski, *passim*; A.J.Froom, letter to the author; van Emden, p.48.
12 Niven, pp.64-73.
13 Sheppard, *passim*; Lunt, Chapter 17, *passim*.
14 The *Halladale* was originally named the *Antonio Delfino*. After the war she was assigned to the United Kingdom by the Tripartite Commission as a war prize. She was scrapped in 1956; *The Review*, Vol.17.1, p.10.
15 Orchard's diary, May 1915.

CHAPTER 2

MALAYA: THE COUNTRY AND THE EMERGENCY

Note: The map on page 30 shows the Malayan states and towns named in this book.

THE COUNTRY

Malaya is a peninsula stretching for 450 miles south-east from the border with Siam. Its greatest width is 200 miles, and its area is a little larger than that of England. The peninsula has a backbone of jungle-covered mountains rising to 7,000ft. In the 1950s four-fifths of the land was evergreen jungle and undergrowth, and the remainder consisted of rubber plantations, rice fields, tin mines, villages and towns.

The south of Malaya lies within 100 miles of the equator, and the average temperature at noon is 90 degrees Fahrenheit, with little variation throughout the year. Most parts of the country receive between 90in and 100in of rain a year. The level of humidity is high at 80 to 85 per cent, and Europeans find the climate enervating at first. Monsoons affect the east coast from November to March, and the rest of the country from June to September. The nights are usually clear and around 20 degrees cooler than the days, depending on altitude. Towards morning, mists form in valleys and sheets of cloud mantle the mountains. As the sun rises the clouds dissolve, but by noon cumulus cloud begins to form, and by late afternoon thunderstorms lasting up to half an hour often occur.

One of the more detailed descriptions of primary jungle, which covers ground which has never been cleared, was written by Lieutenant-Colonel Spencer Chapman DSO, who spent three and a half wartime years living amidst this vegetation:

> Up to a height of ten feet or so a dense undergrowth of young trees and palms of all kinds hid the roots of the giants, but out of this wavy green sea

> of undergrowth a myriad tree-trunks rose straight upwards with no apparent decrease in thickness ... for a hundred or a hundred and fifty feet before they burgeoned into a solid canopy of green which almost entirely shut out the sky. Next to the remarkable symmetry of the tree-trunks, the most astonishing thing was the amount of parasitic growth. Many of the boles of the trees were almost hidden by a network of creepers... In other places the vines and creepers hung straight down from the branches to the ground, where they had taken root again and looped themselves from tree to tree like the crazy rigging of a thousand wrecked ships. Up in the tree-tops where the great trunks suddenly burst into branches were huge hanging gardens of mosses and ferns, whose rotting foliage seemed to provide its own soil.[1]

Chapman's description does not apply to all primary jungle because the shade cast by the tree canopy often prevents the growth of bushes which form the undergrowth. He omitted to mention the presence of fallen giant trees, usually brought down by storms, which obstructed the progress of troops unless they had fallen in the same direction as they were heading and could thus be clambered up and walked along as if they were bridges. The fall of these trees enable shafts of sunlight to reach the ground which germinates seeds and stimulates the growth of bushes and young trees, which competed with each other to take over from the fallen giants, and this results in clumps of undergrowth. Visibility varies considerably, but is very limited wherever bushes are present. Because of the shade much primary jungle is comparatively cool, and if tracks or ridges can be found it is often not too difficult to traverse except on mountains, swamps or thickets of bamboo and thorns, though the carrying of heavy packs and weapons adds to the fatigue. Wildlife includes monkeys, snakes, tigers, elephants, bears, wild pigs and deer, though the last five species were rarely seen. Insects range in size from large butterflies, moths, dragonflies and beetles to mosquitoes and tiny sand-flies, while leeches inhabit streams, rivers, swamps and the damp jungle floor. Ants occur everywhere, march in long columns, bite like mad and eat everything in sight.

Secondary jungle covers areas which have once been cleared and are in the process of reverting to their original state. Lalang (coarse grass up to 6ft high) and bushes grow in abandoned clearings, and as the bushes develop into small trees, creepers, vines and thorns appear. Lack of a dense tree canopy to block out the sun makes it very hot, and exhausting to try to move through.

Malaya's principal economic resources were rubber and tin, and the bulk of its wealth came from the export of these raw materials. Being situated at one of the great maritime crossroads of the world, the country has long been the meeting place of peoples from other parts of Asia, and so the population has great ethnic, linguistic, cultural and religious diversity. In the early 1950s the population numbered about 6 million, consisting of some 3 million Malays, 2.5 million Chinese, 500,000 Indians (mostly Tamils), possibly 50,000 Aboriginals, 25,000 Europeans and 20,000 Eurasians.

The Malays are a very pleasant people, relaxed, courteous and religious, though the Muslim beliefs of the majority are orthodox and not radical. In the 1950s the majority enjoyed life in their kampongs (villages) where the warm damp climate guaranteed ample food for relatively little effort. The attractive village houses were built on stilts and were made of wood with atap (thatched) roofs. The surrounding paddy fields supplied rice, groves provided coconuts and bananas, and plantations and gardens supplied fruit and vegetables. Water buffalo supplied pulling power, and the jungle provided wild fruits, fish and game. Chickens and ducks supplied eggs and meat. Arriving with my platoon at a Malay village off the beaten track was always a delight for me because of the warm welcome, the delicious curry and the amusing sight of young children gaping at the first white man they had ever seen.

This pleasant gentle life contrasted sharply with that of many Chinese who, not having inherited any land, were tin miners, rubber tappers or vegetable gardeners eking out a subsistence level existence, many on land on the jungle edge owned by the Malay Sultans, which the poor people were occupying illegally. The authorities called them 'squatters', and most of them had moved there during the war to escape Japanese brutality. Other Chinese lived in the towns and were wealthy entrepreneurs who controlled a much larger part of the business and industrial economy than the more numerous Malays, who were less attracted by the hard work in towns needed to acquire wealth.

The majority of the Indians were labourers on plantations and roads, though there was an educated class employed as clerks or in professions. Sikhs acted as guards for the larger shops and banks, sitting on beds on the pavement outside the premises with their shotguns propped alongside as they chatted to friends. It was thought that they earned their money not by stopping raids on the shops they were supposedly guarding but through their protection squads which tracked down any robbers and exacted revenge.

There were several Aboriginal tribes living in the deep jungle. In the north were the Negritos, a race of Negroid pygmies, and in the south were the Proto-Malays, a racial mixture speaking an archaic form of Malay. In between were the Senoi, who were divided into two sub-groups, the Temiar in the north and the Semai in the south. The material life of these primitive people had never advanced, and the men spent much of their time hunting with blow-pipes and poisoned darts, or with bows and arrows.

British involvement in Malaya had begun in 1786 as a result of the need to establish trading posts to handle exports from Britain and India and imports from the Far East, and naval bases from which British fleets could operate

Malaya – states and towns named in the text.

against the French or the Dutch in times of war. Trading posts and ports were established by the English East India Co. in the Straits of Malacca by treaty with the Malay rulers of Penang (in 1786) and Singapore (in 1819). The town of Malacca was ceded to Britain by Holland in 1825. These three became known as the Straits Settlements.

In the nineteenth century the Malay States on the mainland suffered much unrest and civil strife, and enjoyed no real law and order. From the

1820s large numbers of Chinese began arriving to work in the tin mines, and later large numbers of immigrants arrived from India and Ceylon to work on plantations and in towns. Disputes over succession to the Sultanates, arguments over taxes, piracy and smuggling on the coast, and civil wars among Malays, or among Chinese, or between Malays and Chinese, were frequent. This unrest adversely affected the business of the merchants of the Straits Settlements, and they began to clamour for the intervention of Britain. Fears of intervention by other European powers also played a part in the British decision to get more involved in Malaya.

Intervention was complicated by the fact that each of the nine Malay States was ruled by its own Sultan (or by a Raja in the case of Perlis) so multiple negotiations were needed to obtain countrywide agreements. In 1874 British residents were accepted by the Sultans of Perak, Selangor and Negri Sembilan, and in 1888 a British Adviser was accepted by the Sultan of Pahang. In 1896, these four central States became known as the Federated Malay States (FMS). The two remaining areas then outside British control were the southern State of Johore (which was already economically linked to the Straits Settlement of Singapore) and the States of Kedah, Perlis, Kelantan and Trengganu in the north, which were under Siamese influence until 1909 when Britain took over. These five States accepted British Advisers, but they did not join the centralised administration of the FMS, so became known as the Unfederated Malay States (UMS).

Unification of the country under British rule was finally completed in 1946 when the Federation of Malaya was formed by amalgamating the FMS, the UMS, and the Straits Settlements of Penang and Malacca. Singapore, with its predominantly Chinese population, was not included in the Federation. The Federal government was headed by a British High Commissioner, and there was a Federal Legislative Council of official and nominated members. Each of the nine States had a Malay Sultan or Raja, a Malay Chief Executive and a British Adviser. These were the governmental arrangements in place when the Emergency began in 1948.[2] From 1952 to 1954, General Sir Gerald Templer was both High Commissioner and Supreme Head of the Armed Forces.

The Background to the Emergency

The Malayan Communist Party (the MCP) was set up in 1930 as one of the bodies intended to help achieve the long-term aim of the Soviet Union, which was to establish communist states throughout the world.[3] Among those present at the formation of the party was Ho Chi Minh, who had also been a founder member of the French Communist Party and later became the leader of the Viet Minh.[4] Malayan Chinese always formed at least 90 per cent of the membership of the MCP as few Malays or Indians supported communism, largely because of their religious beliefs.

In 1932 the British Special Branch in Singapore had a major stroke of luck when they recruited a man called Lai Te who, six years later, became leader of the MCP.[5] Lai was an extraordinary person, and many aspects of his life (and death) remain a mystery to this day. He was Vietnamese, and appears to have begun his career as an agent of the French in Indo-China until his cover was 'blown' and he was recruited by a Special Branch officer who was visiting Saigon. Brought to Singapore, he joined the MCP, claiming that he was a member of the Comintern who had studied communism in Russia and France, had assisted the Vietnamese Communist Party in its early struggles, and had served on the Shanghai Town Committee of the Communist Party of China. These claims (which were not investigated by the MCP until after the war) and his organising ability, led to promotion within the party. The MCP had been declared illegal by the Singapore authorities, and in 1934 Lai fed information to Special Branch which enabled them to arrest and deport to China the whole of the party's Central Committee. With so many of the party hierarchy removed, Lai rose rapidly through the ranks, and in 1938 became their leader. His subsequent career, and the reputed circumstances of his death, are described later in this chapter. Until 1941 the MCP had pursued a policy of fomenting strikes to weaken the British colonial government, but this changed overnight on 22 June when Germany invaded Russia and supplies of tin and rubber were required for the war effort of that communist country.

On 8 December 1941, the Japanese landed in south Siam and north Malaya and began an advance to the south which culminated in the capture of the so-called impregnable fortress of Singapore seventy days later, when more than 130,000 of our soldiers surrendered. Our army had outnumbered the Japanese by about two to one throughout the campaign, but the enemy had more and better aircraft, and more than fifty tanks, while our troops had none.[6] The surrender was the greatest national humiliation suffered by Britain since Yorktown, and the major share of the blame rests on successive pre-war British governments which failed to develop adequate armed forces and defences.[7] As early as 1912, General Sir Ian Hamilton had reported that as Singapore had no landward defences it was vulnerable to attack from a potentially hostile Japan, but his warning was ignored.[8] Nevertheless, had the British military commanders in Malaya performed well when the Japanese invaded then the tragedy would certainly have been delayed, and possibly even averted had sufficient troop and aircraft reinforcements been sent in time. The importance of hindsight must be recognised when criticising leaders who encountered unexpected problems such as the skill of the Japanese soldiers and pilots, the availability of their tanks and the number and quality of their aircraft, but many of the British misjudgements seem inexcusable, and a few of these are now described.

The C-in-C Far East refused permission for the Army to cross the Siamese border until it was too late to oppose the invader at the narrow isthmus just north of the border, which was the only possible place where a successful defence could have been mounted. The C-in-C was afraid that an early crossing would offend the Siamese, but as Japan already controlled the Siamese government, offending them would have been of no importance.[9] The close relationship between Japan and Siam was demonstrated in 1943 when the former promised to hand over to the latter the four northern Malay States of Perlis, Kedah, Kelantan and Trengganu.[10]

There were two actions the GOC Malaya should have taken to hold up the Japanese advance until adequate reinforcements arrived. He should have concentrated all his forces in the west of the country where the main Japanese attack was taking place, and he should have built defences in south Malaya behind which the Army could have retired to hold up the enemy's advance. He did neither.[11]

The C-in-C Eastern Fleet believed that aircraft could not sink capital ships while they were at sea, despite having received warnings to the contrary. He sailed the battleship *Prince of Wales* and the battle cruiser *Repulse* in search of Japanese invasion convoys, and both were sunk by torpedo bombers. Although the RAF's aircraft did not match those of the Japanese in quality or quantity, it seems extraordinary that these valuable ships were not provided with any air cover whatsoever, and that our first aircraft to come on the scene arrived only just in time to watch the *Prince of Wales* go down. This disaster cost the Royal Navy one of the only two modern battleships it had at the time, and the lives of 840 men.[12]

The errors committed by GHQ during the campaign have been summed up by Major-General Woodburn Kirby, the principal author of volume I of the official *History of the War against Japan*:

> Those responsible for the conduct of the land campaign in Malaya committed every conceivable blunder. They underrated their enemy, they paid insufficient attention to the training of their troops, and they delayed taking urgent decisions even after the Japanese had landed.[13]

A useful source of information about the activities of the MCP during the war is Spencer Chapman, who knew Lai Te and his successor Chin Peng, and trained some members of the party who went into the jungle at the time of the Japanese invasion, and who after the war became terrorists in 1948. Chapman had been posted to Singapore in September 1941, and took command of the Special Training School (101st STS) which had been set up to train guerillas to stay behind the lines of enemy invaders in the

Far East. After the Japanese invaded he went into the jungle with some compatriots, and stayed there until May 1945 when he was evacuated by submarine to Ceylon. By the time of the British surrender of Singapore in 1942, 165 MCP members had been trained at STS and sent up country to set up camps in the jungle. They became the nucleus of what the MCP later named the Malayan People's Anti-Japanese Army (the MPAJA), which eventually numbered some 5,000 men.[14] These guerillas carried out few attacks on the occupying Japanese, but concentrated on killing collaborators, fighting Kuomintang guerillas who supported Chiang Kai Shek, staying alive, receiving training and weapons from the British and preparing to seize power when the war ended.

Spencer Chapman subsequently wrote a very successful book entitled *The Jungle is Neutral* describing his wartime adventures. The title resulted from his belief that as the jungle provided unlimited cover for both friend and foe, it was neutral.[15] Its neutrality, however, really depended on the relative abilities of the friend and the foe to take advantage of its cover and to cope with the problems it caused. Malayan Chinese terrorists with years of jungle experience were rather better at exploiting the cover than British troops who had recently arrived in the country, and who spent much of their time in camps outside the jungle. A doubt about the accuracy of Chapman's reporting of some of his amazing wartime exploits resulted from his reputation for exaggeration which he had acquired during his expedition to Greenland in 1930. His colleagues had invented the dictum 'divide by two and call it nearly' to apply to his claims of the distances he had trekked through the snow covered terrain. This saying was resurrected by those who doubted his later claim to have made the first ascent of the 24,000ft-high mountain of Chomolhari in Tibet in 1937, and by those who queried his account of some of his solo adventures in wartime Malaya.[16]

Soon after the Japanese occupied Singapore they arrested Lai who, to save his life, became their agent. He gave them information which enabled them to arrest and execute all the other MCP leaders in Singapore, and to kill most of a group of their MPAJA leaders who were operating in the jungles of mainland Malaya and were meeting at Batu Caves near Kuala Lumpur. Lai had an effective technique for getting rid of those colleagues he thought were too ambitious, or suspicious or critical of his policies, or those whose betrayal was demanded by his Japanese masters. He summoned them to a meeting, informed the Japanese of its time and place, and failed to turn up himself having supposedly been delayed en route. He drove a car freely throughout Malaya during the Japanese occupation, and the failure of the surviving party leaders to become suspicious of his apparent amazing luck remains a mystery.

Lai kept in touch with his previous employers during the Japanese occupation by visiting British officers from Force 136 (part of the Special Operations

Executive), who had been landed by submarine in Malaya from Ceylon in 1943 and were encamped in the jungle engaged, with Spencer Chapman, in training the MPAJA. When long-range aircraft based in Calcutta became available in November 1944, airdrops of arms began. With the benefit of hindsight it would, of course, have been better if we had not trained and armed the MPAJA since we never needed their assistance to support our return to Malaya in September 1945 as the Japanese had surrendered the previous month. What is more, those involved in training the communists knew that their post-war aim was to take over the country by force. We made a similar error of judgement late in the war by setting up a Jewish Brigade in the Army. It fought the enemy for only six weeks, and before being demobilised its soldiers smuggled illegal immigrants and stolen weapons into Palestine to prepare for the Jewish struggle against the British, who were responsible for the country under a League of Nations mandate.[17]

The British intended to liberate Malaya ('Operation Zipper') by landing our forces in the south-west of the country, and through the efforts of my friend General Ibrahim, the Japanese had been misled into thinking that we were going to land in the north-west and had moved many troops to strengthen their defences there. My letter of 10 July 1953 and accompanying notes in Chapter 3 give details of Ibrahim's achievement. The only amusing feature of 'Zipper' was that it was originally intended to have been accompanied by the seizure of the Siamese island of Phuket in an operation appropriately code-named 'Roger'.[18]

After the British return, Lai resumed contact with Special Branch in Singapore. He had simultaneously been a communist leader, and an agent of both the Japanese and the British; few spies have ever succeeded in helping three opposing military powers at the same time with such success. His family life was also unusual, with three or four Vietnamese and Chinese wives and a one-handed but beautiful Vietnamese mistress.[19] What a fascinating book this man could have written!

The more militant members of the MCP wanted to use the MPAJA to try to take over the country immediately after the end of the war, and before the British Army returned to Malaya the towns of Bentong, Raub, Kuala Lipis and Jerantut, all in Pahang, fell into the hands of the communists.[20] The MPAJA also took the opportunity to kill many citizens who they expected would oppose communism in the future.[21] Their occupation of the towns did not last long as the British returned in considerable force, and Lai, perhaps acting on the instructions of Special Branch, was not planning an immediate insurgency. The majority of the MPAJA members disbanded on Lai's orders, received a small gratuity from the British, and handed in most of the arms they had received by airdrop. Several thousand guerilla leaders and men remained hidden in the jungle with buried arms dumps containing large numbers of weapons. These arms consisted of those abandoned by the British Army during its defeat by the Japanese, those airdropped into the jungle and deceitfully declared 'not found' by the MPAJA, and those abandoned by the Japanese when they surrendered. Instead of launching an immediate insurgency the MCP adopted a programme of organising strikes and civil unrest to weaken the colonial government while awaiting a suitable moment to begin their armed struggle.

Doubts among the MCP's members about Lai's loyalty were first aired in September 1945 when a party member who had been a Japanese agent in Singapore during the occupation denounced him as a traitor in an article in a Penang newspaper, but this was largely ignored because its author was known to have been an enemy agent.[22] Some members thought Lai's policies were too right wing, and criticised him for allowing most of the MPAJA to disband after the war. A meeting of MCP leaders was called for 6 March 1946 to discuss these matters, but Lai failed to appear and vanished with the party's funds. His successor, Chin Peng, estimated these funds to have amounted to almost 2 million Malayan dollars (£250,000), but what happened to the money remains a mystery.

Chin Peng's account of events after Lai disappeared is as strange as the story of Lai's previous life. Chin went to Bangkok to brief the Siamese communists about the renegade. He claimed that while riding in a trishaw he spotted Lai buying cigarettes from a roadside vendor, but he vanished before Chin could approach him. The Siamese communists later told him that they had tracked Lai down, strangled him, and dumped his body in a river. At the time Chin was merely told that Lai was dead, all details of his death being withheld, and he did not learn about them for another three years.[23] As the Siamese communist leaders must have been told that Lai had absconded with large sums of money, why was he supposedly killed without being made to reveal the whereabouts of these funds? Given Lai's long experience of keeping his movements secret, the help in escaping from Malaya he must have received from Special Branch, and the money in his possession, the claim that he was assassinated seems unlikely. Why would he risk visiting a country which had communist killer squads? A new identity in a safe country such as Australia seems to be a more likely outcome than a death at the hands of the Siamese.

Shortly before Lai absconded his then number two, Chen Yong, resigned from the MCP having become disillusioned with party policy. In 1948 he was arrested by Special Branch and was quickly persuaded to collaborate. He interrogated captured terrorists, persuaded some of them to become government agents, and supplied psychological profiles of all the MCP hierarchy. He worked for Special Branch for almost ten years, and when his usefulness ended he was sent to Australia with his family. In 2003 he was still alive and living under an assumed name in Melbourne.[24] Chen Yong's assisted move to Australia supports my suggestion that Lai may have received similar help from Special Branch.

Chin's subsequent investigation of Lai's past revealed that his pre-war claims of Comintern and Chinese experience were false. His disappearance was a disaster both for the MCP and for the British. The morale of the party's members was shattered by the treachery, and they began to question the loyalty of their other leaders. The British lost their prime source of information on the plans of the communists, and their control of the person who had most influence over those plans. Lai was replaced as Secretary General of the MCP by Chin Peng, who would lead the party throughout the whole of the Emergency and for many years afterwards.

Chin had been born in 1924 in Sitiawan, in north-west Malaya, where his father (who had been born in China) ran a small business dealing in car and bicycle parts. An avid reader, Chin spent the whole of his summer holiday in 1938 reading books on Marxism which had been lent to him by a Chinese schoolmaster. He became committed to communism and joined the MCP in January 1940. He believed that:'conversion to communism ... provides a faith and belief in a system which, at least to the convert, appears as the incontrovertible true path to what is right and fair among human beings.'[25]

Despite his youth, Chin rose rapidly through the ranks of the party, and after wartime experience with the MPAJA and liaison work with British officers from Force 136, he became party leader in 1946 at the age of twenty-two.

Although he was clearly a dedicated communist, details of his political opinions did not become known to the general public until 2003 when, at the age of seventy-nine, he published a book entitled *My Side of History*. This book should have made a valuable contribution to our knowledge of the Emergency, but unfortunately it has some major weaknesses. The contents were 'as told' to a pair of Singapore-based co-authors, but how much of the material emanated from Chin and how much from his co-authors is not revealed. Chin's failure to quote written sources for many of his statements makes their accuracy uncertain, and without these records he must have relied on his memory of events which took place up to fifty-five years earlier.

The major weakness of the book, however, is that it is full of unsubstantiated criticism of British colonialism and praise of international communism. As he is unable to quote any evidence of the virtues of the latter, the question arises as to why did he become and remain a communist? The only answer that emerges from the book is that he hated colonialism, and admired the works of Marx and Mao Tse Tung, and embraced communism without ever considering whether it had any faults. This is an understandable course of action for a young man, but he did not change his mind even when, in his forties and living in China, he had personal experience of brutal communist policies such as the Cultural Revolution. A critique of his book, and an assessment of its author, are given in Chapter 7.

The disappearance of Lai, and the failure of the programme of civil unrest to bring down the colonial government, led the MCP, early in 1948, to decide to start an armed insurrection with the guerillas and weapons they then had hidden in the jungle. They began recruiting more supporters to train as guerillas and were confident that they could take over the country. When the Japanese surrendered in August 1945, the MPAJA had emerged from the jungle to a hero's welcome from the Malayan Chinese civilian population, who naturally gave them all the credit for having defeated the brutal occupiers as no British soldier appeared in the country until September. Our defeat by the Japanese in 1942 had had a disastrous affect on our reputation and many Malayan Chinese civilians held us in low regard. The MCP devised a slogan for circulation among their members and supporters.[26] This was:

> One Japanese soldier was better than ten British soldiers.
> One MPAJA fighter could resist ten Japanese soldiers.

The logical conclusion to be drawn by anyone who believed this propaganda was that the MPAJA could easily defeat the British, but the claims made in the slogan were, of course, flawed. The British forces had certainly outnumbered the Japanese, though by nearer two to one than ten to one. The MPAJA, though admittedly outnumbered by the Japanese by perhaps ten to one, spent nearly the whole of their time avoiding contact with them, so the word 'resist' is misleading and would more accurately have been replaced by 'evade'. Nevertheless, the partial truths of the slogan made the MCP and their supporters confident of success.

The communists had no radio transmitters, and problems with communications between their political and military leaders (which were to continue to plague them throughout the Emergency) and lack of discipline amongst their lower ranks, resulted in the insurrection starting prematurely on 16 June 1948 when three British planters were murdered, and a State of Emergency was declared by a reluctant High Commissioner two days later. Although the government's reason for adopting the word 'Emergency' instead of 'War' to describe the insurgency is understandable, it meant that the conflict, which lasted for twelve years and cost the lives of more than 12,000 people, was never accurately described.[27] In the Korean War the British Army had 1,078 men killed; during the Malayan Emergency the Army and police had 1,860 men killed.[28] One practical consequence of the use of the term 'Emergency' was that captured terrorists did not qualify as prisoners of war under the Geneva Convention, and so could be executed after trial if found guilty of offences such as carrying weapons. Despite this governmental power only 226 of the 1,296 captured terrorists were hanged during the Emergency.[29]

At first the British authorities labelled the insurgents 'bandits', but because both the Japanese and Chiang Kai Shek had used this term to describe their Chinese communist opponents, and both had lost their wars against them, it was thought that the Malayan Chinese might assume that the British would lose too, so the label was changed to 'communist terrorists'. Because the word 'bandits' continued to be used in my battalion and widely throughout the Army, I used it in my letters home, though for reasons I described in my letter of 10 July 1953 in Chapter 3, I did not think it was an appropriate term. In this book I use the word 'terrorists', except in the extracts from my letters.

The British authorities in Malaya faced many problems in the early days of the Emergency. Post-war demobilisation had significantly reduced the number of British soldiers in the country, and most of the ten remaining battalions were under strength and untrained in jungle warfare. The imposition of a new constitution which had stupidly been drawn up by our Foreign Office without consulting the Malay Sultans had reduced the popularity of the British among the ethnic Malays who had a deep respect for these traditional rulers and religious leaders. The seizure of power by the communists in China in 1949 had raised the possibility of Chinese help for the MCP and increased the fears of the non-communist Malayan Chinese that the MCP would succeed in taking over Malaya, and this made them reluctant to help the authorities by supplying information. The country's economy was suffering from the damage done to rubber estates and the equipment of tin mines during the war. The administration was rent by ill feeling between those British civil servants who had escaped from the country when the Japanese invaded and had returned after the war, and those who had stayed in the country and had been imprisoned for more than three years under appalling conditions. The latter criticised the former for escaping, though it is difficult to see what harm escaping had done to anyone. The police were under strength, and morale was low among the British officers because of fears about promotion prospects after many British new recruits arrived from the recently disbanded Palestine Police Force and were themselves promoted. The incompetence of some senior British officials was demonstrated by the dismissal of the first two Police Commissioners who held office during the Emergency together with the head of the Intelligence Services. When the Emergency began the then High Commissioner was about to be relieved of his post for having lost the confidence of the expatriates, but he died in a plane crash over London on his way home to be dismissed.

Early in 1949 the terrorists restyled themselves the Malayan Races Liberation Army (the MRLA). This name was misleading because less than

10 per cent of their members were Malays or Indians, so the words 'Malayan Races' gave a deceptive picture of the overwhelmingly ethnic Chinese membership of their forces. Had they won, the word 'Liberation' would have meant 'communist dictatorship', with all its resulting horrors. The terrorists enjoyed many advantages. The jungle provided magnificent cover for their camps, whose location was unknown to the authorities, and which were very difficult to find on the ground and virtually impossible to locate from the air. The hard core of the terrorists had been trained and armed by the British during the war and had learned how to evade Japanese troops who were searching for them in the jungle. They had plenty of weapons hidden in arms dumps. They also had the support of many of the 600,000 or so Chinese 'squatters' who lived scattered along the jungle edge. These people, called 'Min Yuen' ('Masses Movement') by the MCP, supplied the terrorists with money, food, medicines, clothes, information, couriers and recruits, and were virtually impossible for the security forces to identify because nearly all wore no uniforms and looked exactly the same as innocent vegetable growers and rubber tappers. As the Min Yuen lived on the jungle edge, communication between them and the terrorists was easy, and the authorities found it almost impossible to prevent them from handing over supplies and information. In 1951 it was estimated that 5,500 members of the Min Yuen were armed.[30]

Under the Emergency regulations only members of the security forces and Aborigines were permitted to be in the jungle, and soldiers were thus allowed to kill anyone else they found there on the assumption that they were terrorists. Unfortunately, some innocent villagers could not resist going in to gather wild fruits or to hunt, and were shot by Army patrols who assumed they were terrorists – no courts martial followed such incidents as the victims had acted illegally. This may sound brutal, but in dense undergrowth soldiers could not risk ordering unidentified people to halt to be questioned because if they were terrorists they would open fire without warning.

In addition to the Min Yuen the terrorists had the support of many of the 50,000 or so Aborigines who lived in the deep jungle. During the war the MPAJA had used these people to grow food and give advance warning of the arrival of Japanese troops, and during the Emergency the terrorists continued to receive their help, either voluntarily or as a result of coercion. These primitive child-like people were easy to mislead and intimidate, and the terrorists told them that they had defeated the Japanese and would soon defeat the British. Every time British aircraft flew over the jungle the terrorists told the Aborigines that the planes belonged to them.[31] Like jungle animals, these people had keen senses which could detect soldiers moving through the undergrowth a long way off. Whenever they did so they would vanish without being seen or heard by the troops, and run to warn the terrorists who would quickly evacuate their camps.

Acts of terrorism were easy to carry out and almost impossible to prevent. Most railways and roads at some point on their routes ran through the jungle so trains could be derailed and machine-gunned, and vehicles ambushed. British planters and mine managers and their families living in remote bungalows miles from any police or army post could be murdered, rubber trees could be slashed (more than one million were slashed in 1951), rubber stolen and sold to raise funds for the MCP, workers threatened and informers killed.[32] Village police stations could be attacked and weapons and ammunition seized from the terrified occupants. After each of these incidents the terrorists would vanish into the jungle, nearly always without having suffered any casualties. Follow-ups by the security forces rarely caught anyone because the terrorists usually had several hours' start and could have gone in any of several directions.

To the British, the irony of the Emergency was that we were now trying to kill the same people we had trained and armed during the war, and had decorated, rewarded and fêted after VJ Day. A contingent of the MPAJA had marched in the Victory Parade in London in 1945 where they were inspected by the Queen. Another contingent was presented with campaign medals by Lord Louis Mountbatten in a ceremony in Singapore, where they were accommodated in the famous Raffles Hotel. Chin Peng was mentioned in despatches and awarded an OBE, though this latter honour was later cancelled. One wonders what idiot had decided that this award should be made to a man who had dedicated his life to the forcible destruction of the British Empire. In 1951, Sir Henry Gurney, the High Commissioner, was killed in an ambush organised by Siew Ma who had been trained at Spencer Chapman's STS in Singapore in 1942.[33] How would his widow have felt had she known that her husband's killer had been taught how to ambush him by the British Army?

The irony struck me with considerable force one night during an operation in 1954 when I was reading Spencer Chapman's book *The Jungle is Neutral* by the light of a torch while camped on the bank of the Sungai Mengkuang River. Looking at one of his maps in the book which plotted his wartime treks through the jungle, I saw that he had camped at the site of my present camp. Turning to the chapter which described his visit to this area, I learned that he had come here to train 160 men of the MPAJA.[34] How many of those men were still alive, I wondered, and how many were still in hiding nearby? Would I soon be shooting some of Chapman's old friends, or would they soon be shooting me? I switched off my torch, shut the book, summoned my sergeant and told him to double the number of sentries we had posted round our camp.

The first five years of the Emergency had been particularly difficult for the authorities, but by 1953 the situation had improved. General Sir Gerald Templer had been appointed High Commissioner and Supreme

Commander of the Armed Forces the previous year, and he energetically directed the campaign against the terrorists. Some 563,000 squatters had been removed from the jungle edge and relocated in 535 'New Villages' which were protected by high wire fences, perimeter lighting and Home Guards, and this did much to reduce (but not eliminate) the supplies reaching the terrorists.[35] Security force numbers had increased dramatically. Army strength had more than doubled to twenty-three infantry battalions, and the truly Commonwealth nature of the fight against terrorism was demonstrated by the nationality of the troops now involved – British, Malay, Gurkha, African and Fijian. Convoys were escorted by armoured cars, and spotter aircraft searched for terrorist cultivations in the jungle. Suspected terrorist camps were shelled by artillery, bombed or rocketed by the RAF and (occasionally) bombarded by naval ships in coastal waters. Numbers of regular police had quadrupled to 37,000, and some 34,000 Special Constables and 210,000 Home Guards had been recruited (though only 50,000 of the latter were on duty and armed at any one time).[36]

And at midnight on 16 April 1953, Second Lieutenants John Chynoweth and Simon Pritchard crossed the causeway from Singapore into Malaya.

Notes

1 Spencer Chapman, *The Jungle*, p.34.

2 Gullick, *passim*; Kennedy, *passim*.

3 Most British authors use this name and abbreviation to describe the party, but most Chinese authors describe it as the Communist Party of Malaya (the CPM).

4 A. Chin, p.22.

5 This man's name has been spelled in a variety of ways, and he used many aliases, but the name Lai Te was used by his successor Chin Peng, so has been adopted here.

6 Keegan, pp.257, 261.

7 Kirby, *Singapore*, pp.xiii, 254.

8 Lee, p.116.

9 Kirby, *The War*, p.61.

10 Allen, p.164.

11 Kirby, *Singapore*, p.251.

12 Middlebrook, pp.58-59, 252-53, 284, 314.

13 Kirby, Singapore, p.151.

14 Chin Peng, p.125.

15 Spencer Chapman, *The Jungle*, p.118.

16 Barker, pp.89, 155.

17 Delano, pp.34-37.

18 Ziegler, pp.297, 300-01.

19 Chin Peng, p.178.

20 Miller, *Menace*, p.51.

21 R. Thompson, p.15.

22 Miller, *Menace*, p.62.

23 Chin Peng, pp.184, 187-91.

24 Ibid., pp.174, 224-25

25 Ibid., Chapter 3, *passim*.

26 A. Chin, pp.29-30.

27 Estimates made by the present author based on Short, pp.507-08. About 7,500 terrorists, 1,900 soldiers and policemen, and some 3,000 civilians died. These figures include my estimates of the number of those who died of wounds, and civilians who were missing and probably murdered.

28 *The Daily Telegraph*, 7 February 2005, p.9 (Korea); Short, pp.507-08 (Malaya).

29 Short, pp.384, 507-08.

30 Barber, pp.17, 123.

31 In the early days of the Emergency, the terrorists also used this tactic to mislead Chinese peasants in remote villages: Short p.103.

32 Gullick, p.98.

33 Chin Peng, pp.191-2, 287.

34 Spencer Chapman, *The Jungle*, pp.125, 183-85.

35 Short, p.391, footnote.

36 Postgate, p.160.

CHAPTER 3

JUNGLE TRAINING AND OPERATIONS: 16 APRIL–4 AUGUST 1953

Note: This, and the next two chapters, contain extracts from the sixty-eight letters describing the author's twenty operations which involved 115 days in the jungle. Extracts from the letters are presented here in typewriter font. In 1953 a Malayan dollar was worth *2s 4d* in sterling, or 11½p in current UK currency. In 1953 a pound sterling had approximately twelve times the purchasing power of a pound sterling in 2004.[1]

16 APRIL 1953, WITH SIMON PRITCHARD ON THE NIGHT TRAIN FROM SINGAPORE TO SEREMBAN IN MALAYA

We were issued with revolvers and ammunition, a very peculiar feeling sleeping with a loaded gun under one's pillow, and armed guards in the corridor, and a pilot train leading.

The 'pilot train' was probably a Wickham trolley – a large enclosed armoured wagon intended to protect trains if the track had been sabotaged.[2]

A truck from Port Dickson met us, and we arrived at the Malay Regiment Depot about 9.00 a.m. The uniform we will wear is very smart - shorts, short-sleeved shirt, Sam Browne belt, green lanyard, brass shoulder flashes, and a green velvet hat. We already know where we are going when we finish our course, me to the 5th Battalion and Simon to 6th. Lucky old me has the best posting according to all accounts, near Penang the holiday resort.

I have had a very charming letter from a captain in the 5th Battalion welcoming me:

'We have had a copy of your posting order, and I'm delighted to see that you are coming to us - you are the first National Service officer that we have ever had.'

Simon is going somewhere in the wilds (Raub). Everyone sympathises with us over our pay position. We get half the regular subalterns' pay, and told we will not be well off. Everybody advises us to sign on for three years - double pay, promotion, loan to buy a car, £300 gratuity, and four month's paid leave in England. I shall do nothing about this.

There are still plenty of bandits, three were killed on the Cameronians' last patrol last week.

The number of terrorists in 1953 is estimated to have been 5,500.[3] The Cameronians killed 125 during their time in Malaya.[4]

However, the information is pouring in, and we'll finish the bastards off fairly soon.

Wrong. Most of the information we received from the police proved to be inaccurate, and the Emergency lasted for another seven years.

The Malay is a charming character, easy-going, polite and always cheerful. I'm looking forward to leading them.

21 APRIL 1953, PORT DICKSON, FIRST JUNGLE TRAINING EXERCISE

We had our first jaunt into the jungle yesterday, about ten miles from Port Dickson. We were driven by lorry to a rubber plantation and set off from there. We had a Malay lieutenant, a Malay sergeant-major and about six privates. We were armed with Mark 2 carbines and Owen guns, and used maps and compasses to reach our objective, a disused sawmill. We waded through lalang (tall grass growing up to six feet high) primary jungle (cutting our way with jungle knives) and finally swamp. Of these the swamp was the most unpleasant. We often sank in up to our waists in thick, smelly mud and rotten vegetation. There is also an unpleasant species of spiked bush that plays hell with your hands and arms. Sweat poured off us continuously, and flakes of dead wood floated in the air and stuck to you.

It took us about two hours to do about two miles, and this apparently was fast going.

We had to keep our eyes skinned for bandits as this is a suspect area, but luckily for us (and them) none showed up. A monkey nearly got a burst of fire from me when I saw a brown arm up a tree! The insect life is teeming and, for me, fascinating. Multi-coloured butterflies flutter, red and purple dragonflies hum, and huge black beetles as big as a match box go buzzing by. I find I want to stop and catch them instead of watching for bandits especially as no bandits have been seen for some time. Still, I shall cure this distressing tendency or someone will cure it for me!

There are more than 800 species of butterflies and 200 species of dragonflies in Malaya.[5] As a schoolboy I had been extremely interested in entomology, and had spent many hours collecting and breeding butterflies and moths.

The worst thing is the discomfort - badly scratched arms, insect bites, soaking clothes, roots that catch you, rotten wood that gives way etc. all makes one furious and bad tempered with others. Still, it's not too bad and very, very interesting.

Mess kit (blue trousers with red stripe, light green sash round waist, white mess jacket with green epaulettes, gold badges and buttons, ooh lah lah!) will be ready in a fortnight. A general in the Brazilian Army has nothing on me, bar pay! Major-General Lancelot Perowne came to lunch the other day. I had to sit bang opposite the old boy who is a typical caricature of a general - eyeglass, moustache, red face, dozens of ribbons. I could barely keep a straight face as he looked as if he'd just stepped out of Punch.

Punch was a popular magazine which specialised in amusing stories about English Society. As we began lunch the general looked round the table and asked: 'Which of you is Chynoweth?' 'I am, Sir', I replied. 'Your posting has been changed', he announced, 'You're now going to 6 Malay.' Simon, whose leg I had been pulling about his ghastly posting to 6 Malay while crowing over my posting to the beach resort, was lifting a soup spoon to his lips when this news emerged and his burst of laughter nearly spattered the general with consommé.

26 APRIL 1953, PORT DICKSON, THE NEW POSTING

Bad news of my posting - am not going to the 5th but to the 6th Battalion, at Raub in the wilds. Less fun and more bandits.

Raub was in the State of Pahang (pronounced Pahung) in the middle of Malaya, and in 1953 it contained more terrorists than any other state.[6]

Did you see that a big bandit was accounted for last week? His men cut his head off and gave themselves up. And head! This shows their morale is very low; they are being starved and hunted, and whereas in 1949 they attacked in company strength (150-200) now they have to split up in twos and threes because they can't get the food for more. This makes them much more difficult to kill.

The 'big bandit', as I inappropriately called him, was 'Shorty' Ah Koek, the commander of the MRLA in southern Malaya. He had a reward of $150,000 (£19,750) on his head if taken alive or $75,000 (£9,375) if killed. As he was only 4ft 9in tall the *Straits Times* newspaper reported that at $3,000 an inch (actually $2,632) he was 'probably the most expensive bandit sought'. Ah Koek had been murdered in October 1952 by his bodyguard of two men and a woman who cut off his head and took it to a police station. The news was kept from the public until April 1953, presumably to prevent his leaders from learning of his death.

Chin Peng claims that the decapitation was contrived by Special Branch to provide the British authorities with an example of a decapitation by terrorists to counter the criticism of the Army then current in Britain for decapitating terrorist corpses for identification purposes. However, he does not explain how Special Branch could have 'contrived' this result.[7]

Food shortages had certainly reduced the size of terrorist groups and made them more difficult to kill, but 'fives and sixes' would have been more accurate than 'twos and threes'.

They are 90 per cent Chinese, and it's thought that one or two Englishmen are leading some platoons; this has never been proved, but there is a strong suspicion. Several men have heard English spoken during a raid: 'Christ, here come the Cameronians, scatter chaps', and one Malay sergeant here has seen a white man leading bandits, a guardsman by his bearing. These are probably deserters.

It was never officially acknowledged that any white man had ever joined the terrorists, but there were many reports that at least one was with them. In 1948 and 1949 a white man was reported in Kedah, and in 1950 one was seen in Perak. The Suffolk Regiment reported seeing one in an ambush party in Selangor, and in 1952 the police reported that one was with terrorists near Tapah. In 1953 some Aborigines reported that a white man with blue eyes and a beard was operating a wireless set in a terrorist camp on the Jelai Kechil river in Pahang.[8] As no Chinese, Malays or Indians had blue eyes and very few Chinese and Malays had beards, this tended to confirm the claim of it being a white man, but as the terrorists had no wireless sets capable of transmitting, this cast doubt on the accuracy of the report. Perhaps the man seen was a British police officer camped with a patrol of Chinese policemen.

At the time it was thought that some of these sightings may have been of Pat Noone, an English anthropologist who had gone into the jungle in 1941 to escape the Japanese invaders, had worked with the MPAJA for a time, and had never emerged at the end of the war. This theory later proved to be wrong, and Noone's life and death are described in the Epilogue. Although these sightings were apparently genuine, they were probably mistaken, because if the MRLA had ever had a white man in its ranks, Chin Peng would almost certainly have boasted about it in his book. It may be that some of those seen were unusually large, pale-skinned Chinese, but still the suspicion remains. During the Second World War Spencer Chapman and his colleagues had demonstrated that it was possible for Englishmen to live in the jungle with Malayan Chinese communists for years while being hunted by enemy troops.

> Getting the Malay officers here to tell of their personal experiences against Japanese, and later against bandits, is fascinating. One of our instructors, Lieutenant 'Busty' Hussein, was a sergeant in the Malay Regiment during the battle of Singapore in 1942, and was captured by the Japanese, escaped, and was captured again and did six months on the Siamese railway, the Railway of Death. I'm surprised he can ever smile again after his experiences there. He escaped again, and became a storeman with the Indian National Army.

Illustration number 5 in the picture section shows a picture of Lieutenant Hussein. The Indian National Army (INA) had been formed by the Japanese, largely from some of the 60,000 Indian Army prisoners of war who had been captured at the fall of Singapore in 1942. These men joined the INA to get better treatment, and in the hope that when the Japanese had won the war they would grant independence to India. In 1943, leadership of the INA was taken over by the Indian revolutionary nationalist, Subhas Chandra Bose.

About 7,000 men of the INA who had been sent to Burma joined Japanese troops in March 1944, in their failed attack on Imphal and Kohima which were fifty miles inside India. The propaganda triumph of having crossed the border into India rapidly turned into a military disaster for the Japanese and the INA as they were soon forced to retreat. Shortly after they surrendered in August 1945, Bose left Singapore in a Japanese plane which crashed in Taiwan, where he died of his injuries. Apparently many Indians believe that Bose is still alive and regard him as a national hero. As many INA men were killed fighting against the British forces (which included very many loyal Indians), and as the British granted independence to India two years after the end of the war, the whole concept of the INA now seems pointless.[9]

Hussein stole and sold a lot of their stores and absconded before every store check, living in the jungle and being hunted by the Japanese and Indians. He did this twice, and then became cook to the Indian National Army general. He stole, and sold, all the regimental silver, and again fled to the jungle where he got malaria and was looked after by an Iban tracker (a Dyak, a primitive Aboriginal race). After the Liberation in 1945 he rejoined the Malay Regiment, was later commissioned and has killed over a dozen bandits. On one occasion they were tipped off about a bandit camp, and while approaching it the bandit sentry fired at five yards range at him with a Tommy gun with a 100 round magazine.

A Tommy gun's magazine actually held only forty-eight rounds.

The gun misfired and Hussein's batman shot and killed him. They surrounded the camp and got eight. He said: 'It was too difficult to restrain the men, so no prisoners were taken', but I don't think he tried very hard!

He always refers to bandits as 'Those bastards' - unusual for a Malay to swear. He also calls the French that because of their reverses in Indo-China. It makes you think when Siam ('Those Siamese bastards') is the only thing between five or six Vietnam divisions and Malaya. The Siamese have a filthy reputation in Malaya. Hussein must sound a very bloodthirsty character - he is, but is also very charming and friendly to us and a constant source of information about the country. There is no man I'd rather have with me if we bumped into any bandits.

4 MAY 1953, PORT DICKSON, JUNGLE TRAINING AND THE NEW POSTING

Very hot and bitten to pieces by red ants. We saw our first leech, an unpleasant looking creature that met a short, sharp end. The ants are the devil. The ground is alive with them, and they drop off trees down one's neck and bite like hell. The only attraction of swamps is the dragonflies, hundreds of them with blue, green, yellow and crimson bodies.

Raub in Pahang, my new posting, is a God-forsaken place half way up a mountain and surrounded by jungle.

Raub was not 'half way up a mountain' but stood at 450ft in a shallow valley – my informant was wrong, but his critical description showed how the depot staff at Port Dickson viewed a posting to 6 Malay!

The area is fairly troublesome as it's difficult to dig the bastards out and so I expect I shall see a lot of the jungle (and few of the bandits, I hope!). I must tell you that all reports from here of the 6th Battalion are bad. The fighting qualities of the troops are good, but the area is not pleasant, and the Colonel is a b...!

Wrong. When Simon and I got to know Lieutenant-Colonel Laugher OBE, MC, the CO of 6 Malay, we found him pleasant to deal with. The fact that we were not career officers liable to be subjected to critical annual reports meant that we were less afraid of him than were the regulars, and after a few months we were able to pull his leg with impunity. Simon even became bold enough to nudge him in the ribs on occasion and ask, 'What about a spot of leave, Colonel?' Our National Service status allowed us to speak our minds about military practices we disagreed with, but our junior rank and short remaining length of service meant that the regulars took little notice of our views on these subjects.

Re Indo-China, the feeling here is that the Siamese are a treacherous crew and politically unstable. The present regime was established by a military coup, and the deposed Prime Minister is now a red co-operator with a puppet 'Free Siam' in the north. He commands considerable support in Bangkok. The Japs showed that no jungle is impenetrable so the position is not rosy - support for the French and a little bit more guts by them seems the best plan. They have their finest troops in Indo-China, but appear to lack spirit.

16 MAY 1953, NIGHT EXERCISE ON CAPE RICHADO, SOUTH OF PORT DICKSON

The whole affair was rather exciting as we had an electric storm during the night. The wind and noise were deafening, and the men were afraid the trees would fall; a few branches did, but no more. We were very tired after a six mile march with full kit back to Port Dickson in the morning through jungle.

A few days later Simon and I left Port Dickson and drove to Raub to report to Battalion HQ before joining our companies. Many years later the Colonel's obituary in the *Daily Telegraph* described him as a legendary character who was invariably accompanied by his dog Bonzo, and that when one met him for the first time he would say: 'My name's Laugher, and this is Bonzo'.[10] His first words to me, however, were slightly different. 'Now Chynoweth,' he said, 'If you disobey my orders, I'll have you posted to some arse-hole of the Empire. If you bounce a cheque, I'll have you court-martialled, and if you touch the adjutant's wife, I'll send you on a parachute course.'

This was not quite what I had expected after listening to lectures on man management at Eaton Hall ('Good to meet you, Chynoweth, glad to have you in the battalion') but it made me keen to meet the adjutant's wife. Alas, before I could do so her husband was posted away, and they left Pahang. The aftermath of this is described in the Epilogue.

En route to Raub we drove through the deserted Chinese town of Tras, whose 2,000 inhabitants had been taken into custody in 1951 for helping the terrorists who had ambushed and killed Sir Henry Gurney, the High Commissioner. The involvement of Tras with terrorism is confirmed by the fact that Chin Peng's wife had, until shortly before the ambush, been living there with the communist underground.[11] On the wall of the town's first abandoned house by the side of the road, a British soldier had painted the greeting:

WELCOME TO THE SHARP END!

This was to remind newcomers like us that we were not heading for a cushy posting.

25 MAY 1953, 5 PLATOON, B COMPANY, 6 MALAY, KUALA LIPIS, PAHANG

The battalion's four rifle companies were based at different locations in Pahang. B Company, to which I was sent, was camped at Kuala Lipis (hereafter called Lipis). Conditions in Pahang when I arrived were described by Harry Miller, a journalist then working for the *Straits Times* newspaper:

> Pahang had opened its battle against its own horde of terrorists in 1953. The 'Battle of Pahang' was afterwards considered to have brought about the beginning of the end of the military war… When Chin Peng had made his headquarters in Pahang the area became the most important in the country in the context of communist strategy… Few people ventured into it by motor-car from the west: it was too dangerous. Kuala Lipis, the capital, was rarely visited by casual visitors; it was very much 'out on a limb' as only one road ran to and from it.[12]

6 Malay was the latest of the Malay Regiment's battalions to have been formed, but because of the way the regiment was being expanded the new battalion's officers and men were not inexperienced in jungle operations. To create new battalions the existing battalions had each been expanded by an additional company. When the time came to form a new battalion, four of the existing battalions held a lottery to decide which one of their five rifle companies would leave to form the new battalion.[13]

Lipis, though then the State capital, was a small town with a largely Chinese population, with shops, a cinema, a bank, a market, and houseboats on the river offering a variety of sexual entertainments. Many of the town's Chinese inhabitants supported the terrorists. It was about thirty miles north of Battalion HQ at Raub, and as one author wrote:

> In 1948 I was in Malaya with my company of Devons in an isolated detachment, many miles from Battalion Headquarters – an enviable state of affairs, as any infantry officer will agree.[14]

Being geographically isolated from HQ limited the amount of interference by the CO and his staff. When I arrived the company's officers were:

Company commander: Major Ian Rosslyn MC, then away ill.
Second in command: Captain Ibrahim bin Ismail MBE, ('Ib'), then away on leave.
Platoon commanders: Lieutenant Thompson, ('Tommy').
Second Lieutenant Froom, ('Tony').

We had a primitive officers' mess built of timber and atap (palm thatch) containing bedrooms and a sitting room, but we used the nearby Brigade HQ officers' mess for meals and a bar.

My arrival at B company was humiliating. During our journey from Port Dickson we had with us another officer who was joining another Malay Regiment battalion, and on leaving the jeep he by mistake took my green velvet uniform hat called a songkok and left his behind. His head was very much larger than mine, so his songkok covered my eyes and rested on my ears. Obviously I could not wear such a monstrosity so I had to fall back on an Australian bush hat which we had been issued with at Port Dickson, though I cannot recall ever having seen anyone else in the regiment wearing one. When I arrived, Tommy and Tony were treated to the appearance of a bespectacled figure wearing a cowboy hat. They have never forgotten this far-from-stirring military sight, and remind me about it when we meet at reunions. I hope the officer who took my songkok suffered a similar embarrassment when he arrived at his battalion with a tiny green velvet pimple perched on top of his fat head.

I interviewed my platoon yesterday for the first time - 40 men. I have a sergeant and a corporal who speak a fair amount of English, and my Malay is improving slowly (no lessons at Port Dickson).

Simon and I had been refused Malay language tuition on the grounds that, being National Service officers, we had only fifteen months left to serve before being demobilised so it was considered to be not worthwhile sending us on a course. We were told to pick up the language as we went along. Our time at Eaton Hall had taught us nothing about jungle warfare and nearly all our month at Port Dickson had been devoted to acclimatisation rather than training in the jungle. I spent more time on the tennis court and in the sea than I did in the jungle or in the classroom. We were also refused permission to attend a course at the Far East Land Forces School of Jungle Warfare, although National Service subalterns in British regiments were allowed to attend. Instead, we were told to read an Army issue handbook entitled 'The Conduct of Anti-Terrorist Operations in Malaya'. Anyone who has been on active service knows that you cannot learn how to command troops in unfamiliar terrain against an unfamiliar enemy from a handbook – a course on the ground run by experienced campaigners is essential.

The net result of all this was that when I went into the jungle with my platoon for my first operation, ten days after arriving at Lipis, I knew very little Malay and had the words for left and right reversed in my mind. I was baffled when I gave the leading scout an order to turn left while on the march and saw him turn right. What would have happened had we been ambushed when only two of my forty men could have understood my orders? Would I have known what orders to give anyway? The operation was intended to catch or kill the leader of the communists and his fifty-strong bodyguards who were (wrongly) reportedly to be in the area. They would probably have enjoyed meeting me! Would an officer who spoke very little English and had received practically no operational training have been allowed to command British troops on active service?

> The sergeant, Manaf, and the corporal, Talib, are 24. The oldest man is 25 and the youngest 18; most are 19 or 20. They come from all over Malaya, from the states of Kelantan (dialect very difficult to follow), Perak, Trengganu, but most from Negri Sembilan. The sergeant has a first class jungle reputation as a killer so I hope No. 5 platoon will do well. I have a batman, a private in my platoon. Local leave here consists of five days every six weeks. Lipis is miles from anywhere, but it's usual to go to Fraser's Hill - cool, fires in evening, but nothing to do, or Kuala Lumpur - cinemas, clubs, etc.

There was a nine-hole golf course at Fraser's Hill, but I had hardly ever played the game.

> I had a letter from a National Service subaltern friend in the Royal Artillery who was stationed on Salisbury Plain. He's right about National Service/Regular feeling. The short service chaps are OK, but it's the Sandhurst regular junior officers who are the bastards. Any snootiness I meet from them I counter by implying that the Army is the resort of those without enough intelligence to get on elsewhere. This is not always true, but is true enough to be effective.

I don't know why some National Service officers encountered problems with our opposite numbers in the Regular Army. The fact that we spent only four months at Officer Cadet Schools before being commissioned whereas the regulars spent eighteen months at Sandhurst may have made the regulars think that we were inadequately trained amateurs. This assessment may have been partly true, but National Servicemen had no say in determining the length of the officer training they received, and unlike nearly all the Sandhurst cadets, we had spent at least two months in the ranks receiving basic training before going to Cadet School. We thus had more experience of dealing with the other ranks than had the regulars who went to Sandhurst straight from school. Over the years the length of time of officer training has varied considerably. In 1914 some men from public schools or universities were commissioned before having received any Army training whatsoever.[15]

> I can't say that I like or understand the average mentality of a regular officer. Bloody minded sums up a number of them. On the other hand I've met some fine chaps - however, they are in the minority, (and this is typical) and not popular with the majority. We have some ex-Indian Army - all reduced, and my opinion of these, even after making allowance for bitterness, is low.

They were reduced in rank after having had to transfer from the Indian Army to the British Army when India was granted independence in 1947. They suffered a double financial blow as British officers in the Indian Army had been paid more than officers of the same rank in the British Army, so no wonder there was 'bitterness'.

2 JUNE 1953, LIPIS

> The whole battalion is co-operating with the Gurkhas and King's African Rifles in a big sweep to find and kill the chief communist in Malaya and 50 bandits known to be encamped in the area (this must be the largest camp in Malaya). A bandit courier surrendered on Sunday and supplied the information, though even he does not know exactly where the camp is, only the area.

We now know that the terrorist leader, Chin Peng, with his politbureau and bodyguard, had in February 1953 moved to the Cameron Highlands, which was outside our operational area.[16] The claim that Chin's camp was still in our area in June was typical of the wrong information supplied by the police to the Army. The courier who supplied the information to the police did not know the camp's location because all terrorist couriers had to use dead letter drops to preserve the secrecy of the location of the recipient of the message they were carrying.

> The Gurkhas and King's African Rifles are advancing up the ridge and trying to contact while 6 Malay will be encamped in defensive positions on the north side of the river waiting for them. The area is thick jungle and A company are going in by helicopter, we march. We leave at 4.00 a.m. tomorrow.

13 JUNE 1953, SUNGAI LIANG RIVER, MY FIRST OPERATION

I returned from the big operation yesterday safe and sound, and no sign of bandits. The Gurkhas and King's African Rifles got about six, but several miles from our position. We were in for eight days and were very dirty and hairy when we came out. The company was split up into platoons about a mile apart along the river. Likely crossing places were ambushed, but the river was low and one could cross almost anywhere.

The nights are pitch black, and insects and monkeys make so much noise that I'm convinced a whole army could cross and no one the wiser. I'm sure this is not the way to get them. We are not fighting an army, but small groups who do not fight pitched battles with hopeful battalions. Bandits can move many times faster than any of our platoons, are clever and desperate and elusive. The best way is to get information from villages or surrendered bandits who lead one to a definite camp.

My views on the errors of GHQ during the campaign are described in Chapter 6, and it is perhaps significant that it took only one operation for me to decide that 'jungle bashing' by large numbers of soldiers without accurate information was a total waste of time. If a raw subaltern could make this accurate assessment after only eight days' experience, why had the Generals not reached the same conclusion after five years?

Am enclosing three leaflets I found in the jungle, dropped by air in likely areas. The first is a safe conduct pass in English, Malay, Chinese, Tamil and Gurkhali.

Unfortunately my parents did not keep the leaflets I sent home, but see Appendix. The leaflets were intended to persuade terrorists to surrender. I am sure that no Gurkha ever joined the terrorists, and I think that the reason for using Gurkhali was to try to contact the few Gurkhas who had stayed in the jungle after our defeat in 1942, and who had remained there as they did not know the war had ended in 1945.

In 1949 a Gurkha patrol came across a Gurkha corporal living in a shack in the jungle who had been left behind with some rations during the retreat from the Japanese in 1942 because he was suffering from malaria. In a month he had recovered sufficiently to look for a safe place in which to settle, and had built his shack. He had been living on wild pig and fish, and did not know the war was over.[17] I was told that he was given a job in his regiment's officers' mess.

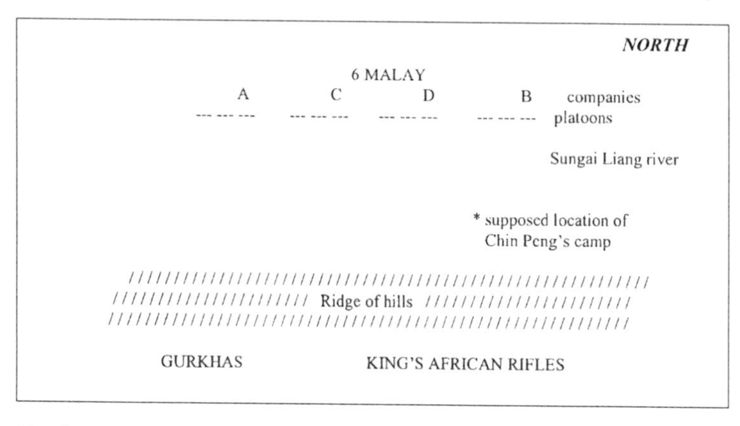

Sketch map of Sungai Liang River Operation.

> The second is a $500 (£58) reward for surrendering, and the third is a general injunction from General Templer to give oneself up.

Leaflets could be found on jungle paths, in deserted terrorist camps and in areas which supported the communists. In 1953 more than 5 million leaflets were airdropped.[18] Aircraft also flew over the jungle broadcasting calls from surrendered terrorists to their comrades to give themselves up. GHQ claimed that in Pahang between June and September 1953 twenty-three terrorists surrendered after reading leaflets, and five after hearing broadcasts from 'voice' aircraft.[19] The accuracy of the first figure is doubtful as the terrorist leaders punished any of their men caught in possession of a leaflet. Chin Peng disputed this last assertion claiming that his commanders allowed safe-conduct leaflets to be carried as life-saving tools.[20]

> Bandits who surrender have a pleasant habit of cutting off a compatriot's head to prove their change of heart, and bringing it in.
>
> We received two airdrops, one by helicopter (food and cigarettes) and one by Dakota (parachute drop of food, boots and socks). These were quite interesting – cutting clearings, using fluorescent panels and smoke bombs to attract attention to one's location. A Malay party of ten men can clear a big area in a short time using parangs (native knives with heavy blades) that go easily through teak trees up to a foot in diameter. The ground was hilly, up to 1,000 feet, and pretty

hard going. I was out on one patrol in which I doubt if we covered more than four miles and yet it took us eight hours with only one ten minute rest every hour (for the benefit of me, the Malay can go on almost indefinitely it seems).

Incidentally, I nearly stopped the whole patrol to go tiger hunting. We cornered one between us and the river, it was ten feet away from me and sounded pretty annoyed about the whole thing, growling and spitting like mad. If I could have found two men willing to come into the bushes with me after it I'd have had a crack at it (we had enough fire power to stop an elephant), but a tiger scares a Malay stiff, and I didn't feel inclined to go in alone. It was only afterwards I remembered we had grenades - a couple in the bushes would have produced some results. I've been kicking myself ever since as I doubt whether I'll ever be so close to one again (they are pretty rare here). Still next time I'll really get on the job with a machine gun, and we'll have a rug yet!

This paragraph made me squirm with shame when I re-read it for the first time fifty years later. The only excuses I can offer are that military training encouraged bloody-mindedness, and that worries about the survival of rare animals had not yet reached me and most other people. I was, however, right in saying that I doubted whether I would ever be so close to one again as I only ever saw one tiger, and that was swimming across a river near Lipis along which I was boating during an operation. When it had climbed up the bank it gave me a casual glance, shook water off itself, and departed into the jungle. One of the few mistakes Spencer Chapman made in describing jungle wildlife was to say that tigers hated to get their feet wet.[21] The opposite is true as 'tigers love water.'[22] The illustration opposite shows a picture of the author on this operation.

I could write a book on leeches and their habits. I seem to have lovely thick blood they go for in a big way, and in rivers and swamps they swarm by the thousand. Taking one's boot off is not pleasant after crossing a river or swamp. It's usually full of blood and bits of burst leech, and one's foot covered in bites that take ages to stop bleeding. Legs and feet suffer most, but <u>every</u> part of one's body is attractive.

A leech in the penis was our greatest fear. We always wondered how the native women could stand for hours up to their waists in water while planting or harvesting rice.

The author, 1953.

> The bite is not painful (that's the trouble, you don't know they are there) and the loss of blood inconsiderable (I suppose) but a more sickening sight I never wish to see. I take no notice now of insect bites (except hornets) but I do draw the line at leeches and burn them off my legs with lighted cigarettes - quite effective though one needs a strong stomach.

I first appreciated the danger of hornets when one of my men walked into a nest and got stung all over his head. His face swelled so much that his eyes, mouth and nostrils closed up, and he could not breathe until we forced a

hollow stem between his swollen lips. It took several painful days before the swelling subsided enough for him to be able to eat.
We found two snakes (both despatched) and I had one unidentified animal in my tent one night (probably a type of rat). I don't know who was more scared, him or me – I nearly took my leg off swiping at it with a kukri (Gurkha knife).

I am ashamed that we killed snakes, of which there were reputedly 130 different species in Malaya.[23] Most were harmless, but we despatched them automatically as if we were swotting flies. The most dangerous snake was the krait, a small black snake with orange bands which lived in the branches of trees. If it dropped on your head and bit you then you would reputedly be dead by the time you hit the ground.

> Some of the streams have a lot of fish in them, and we got a two foot long unidentified fish out of the Sungai Liang with a hand grenade. Quite tasty on a spit (a bigger one was blown to bits).

Although grenades do not make much noise when exploding under water, their use for fishing was banned by the Army. The rule was often ignored even though we were supposed to account for all the grenades we used.

> Our food was twenty-four-hour rations. The Malays had rice and so on, the British officers tinned bacon, beans and the like. Very monotonous, and no fresh food. I perspire much more than the Malays so I drink more. Streams with waterfalls are pretty safe, but the Sungai Liang is white coffee colour. Malays drink it, but I have mine made into tea. We bathed each night in the river (with a Bren gun covering the other bank) and I had one lovely bath in a rock basin with a waterfall into it. It's awkward bathing as the men never bathe in the nude in front of each other, and don't like seeing you in the nude. Awkward because of fiddling round with a towel when balanced on a rock with a carbine in one hand and soap in the other.
>
> It gets dark at 7.30 p.m., and I retire to my tent then, but rarely get to sleep before 11.00 p.m., just lie and think about home comforts, and never walking a step again, and the meal I'm going to have in London when I return, and clean clothes, and no CO's within miles, etc. One advantage of being in the jungle is that one can close down one's wireless set ('Too much interference to hear your order which countermanded the

one you sent yesterday to move to so and so, Sir!') and be one's own master for a few days, and decide where to patrol and when and how.

At Eaton Hall we had been lectured on the importance of using proper signals procedures when transmitting messages by wireless. When contacting Battalion HQ by wireless for the first time, I asked to speak to Sunray Major (the CO), called myself Sunray Minor (a platoon commander) and gave my map reference in code – all this was textbook stuff to preserve the secrecy of our names and ranks and my location. The reply was 'Hello, Chynoweth, Colonel here. I see you are camped near Kampong Kenong'. As the terrorists had no equipment with which to listen to our wireless communications HQ did not bother with measures to preserve security, and nor did I thereafter.

On the first evening of this, my first operation, I joined my sentries in order to find out what it was like being on guard in the jungle at night. I sat with my back to a tree overlooking the river, and as it began to get dark I began to see shadows moving on the far bank. A rising cacophony of sound developed. Chattering chimps? Or chattering Chinks? By the end of my two-hour stint I had seen ten tigers, a dozen elephants, twenty terrorists, and had heard crocodiles splashing in the river and snakes rustling in the bushes. It was the last time I ever joined the sentries.

Simon's experience of his first night in the jungle was far worse than mine. He sleep-walked, woke up somewhere in the undergrowth, and was forced to make pathetic calls like: 'I say, is anyone there?' He was lucky not to have been shot by a sentry before he was found and led back to his tent.

The Malays are fine, my platoon sergeant is excellent. He's killed three bandits and captured one (a woman, who bit him when he grabbed her, much to his annoyance!).

Manaf was later awarded the Military Medal and a mention in despatches.

He speaks fair English and is improving my Malay - we have long talks in Malay and English. Manaf bought his wife for $98 (£11) unseen from her father when she was 15. They exchanged photos, but never met till the wedding day. This is the usual Malay custom, no wonder divorce for Malays consists only of saying 'I divorce thee' three times.

Our company commander, Major Rosslyn MC, is ill, and won't be back for a month or so. Reputedly a man worn out by the jungle, and not easy to get on with.

16 JUNE 1953, LIPIS

Yesterday I had to sit on a court of enquiry for the 3rd Battalion King's African Rifles at Jerantut, 60 miles from here. 'A' company's second in command had lost a month's pay of the company - $4,000 (£466) stolen from the safe after he'd lost the key. We only had to find the facts and give no allocation of blame, but personally I feel he took it himself. Still, even if he didn't he's for the high jump for losing the key. It was quite interesting, specially the African witnesses, pagans who gave a solemn declaration in lieu of the Christian oath on the Bible. They signed their statements with a thumb print as they could not write (some of my men can't read or write either - no schooling during Japanese occupation of Malaya).

26 JUNE 1953, KELAU FOREST RESERVE

We got back yesterday from what proved to be a very exciting operation. Our company was given an area to search in the Kelau Forest Reserve, south of Raub. On the second day out, three bandits walked into the company position, and the leading one was shot dead by a sentry. In spite of vigorous pursuit the others got away. I was searching the top of a hill about 100 yards away at the time, and had just found a large food dump when the bandit was shot. As I tore down the hill towards camp the other two bandits passed me coming up, but the jungle is so thick that I never even heard them although they were not 20 yards away.

I was the first man to reach him. He was a young Chinese of about 20, extremely well dressed in khaki peaked hat with a large red star, khaki jacket, trousers and gaiters, and extremely good boots. He was armed with a German 12 bore shotgun, a very useful weapon in this terrain. He was obviously one of a party carrying food to my food dump - another five minutes and I'd have shot him myself! I have his Chinese compass as a souvenir. The platoon got his watch, Parker 51, two other pens, $5, and other trophies. The food dump was an Aladdin's cave for my men. It was 20 feet up a tree, a Tarzan-like house camouflaged with atap. I, and one of my men, climbed up (a tricky business as there was no ladder), and found 100 yards of khaki cloth, 50 tins of Quick Quaker Oats,

50 tins of Gibbs toothpaste, 50 excellent tooth brushes, writing paper, ink, lighters, lighter flints, towels, underpants, rice (10 stone), Bovril, Marmite, and Brands Essence (for wounded bandits), kerosene oil, and parachute cord (stolen from our airdrops). The scene resembled a pirate share-out and 'LOOT!' was the order of the day. Tuan Snow White (that's me) was trampled in the rush, but by judicious use of his carbine restored enough order to salvage a trifle or two for himself (a dozen towels, etc.).

The value of the stuff was over £100, and a lot more to the bandits who had to run the risk of being caught buying it, manhandle it for five miles over terrible country in small packs (every trip a nightmare of ambush and surprise) and build the house, and hoist it up. My men took all they could carry, and we burned the rest with the kerosene. This sort of thing causes more surrenders than actual killing. A starving bandit arriving at the dump to find it burned must have a morale of below zero.

From then on we found a cultivation (shallots for tea), two camps (deserted) for 40 bandits (including lecture stands, clay ovens, bathing places on the river, machine gun posts) two clearings awaiting cultivation, and numerous fresh tracks - but no more bandits. One of the other platoons found another food dump up a tree and added three bottles of brandy to the loot. One evening I had the pleasure of listening to Radio Malaya (which we can get on our wireless set) announce: 'A very large bandit food dump was found in the Raub area of Pahang yesterday', and that was me (fame at last?).

Chin Peng regularly listened to Radio Malaya on his wireless set, and if he heard the report about the food dump then this would have been the closest contact he and I ever had.[24]

After four days we received a parachute drop of food including 100 oz of rum per platoon, and the men don't drink spirits as they are Mohammedans! We three platoon commanders had a high old time every evening afterwards ('Jungle Juice Cocktail' - take one waterbottle of water, three bars of milk chocolate, melt and stir, add nine rums and shake, allow to cool and drink quickly - keeps the mosquitoes away!).

It was noticeable how good the quality of the bandit supplies and equipment is. The food is British, and they must have the backing of huge sums of money supplied by rich Chinese either freely or by blackmail (freely we suspect). I would trust no Chinese in Malaya. When one finds a track one day old leading right up to the wire fence of a Chinese Village, and receive information that ten bandits picked up food there the night before, one gets mad, all our sweating and suspense in the jungle is wasted unless the civilians co-operate. All my men were livid and begged me to open up with our three Bren guns on the village as a salutary lesson. I lost several stone in restraining them - I'd visions of a court-martial.

By 1953 most Chinese squatters had been re-housed in hundreds of 'New Villages'.[25] These were protected by high wire fences, floodlights and guards, but the terrorists continued to receive support from some squatters.[26] Rice was smuggled out inside bicycle pumps and frames, cigarette tins and in false bottoms of buckets of pig swill. My criticism of the Chinese may seem unduly severe, but more than 90 per cent of the terrorists were of this race, and they continued to be helped by as many as 50,000 Chinese civilian supporters.[27] Illustration number 7 in the picture section shows a Chinese New Village headman whose facial expression does not indicate much liking for the author who took his photograph.

No Chinese rubber tapper is safe when we search an estate, my men are trigger happy with Chinese, and several platoon commanders have had to plant grenades on tappers and call them bandits when their men have made 'a small error in judgement'.

A 'small error in judgement' is a heartless description of the killing of innocent rubber tappers, but our difficulties were illustrated by the experience of a friend. On a rubber estate he stopped a Chinese girl tapper who, in response to his order, lifted off her shoulders the wooden yoke from which hung two buckets of latex. She placed the buckets on the ground, smiled at him, plucked a grenade from one of the buckets and threw it at him. It did not go off, probably because it was old, and she escaped through the jungle edge while he and his patrol took cover behind tree trunks to avoid the expected explosion.

Part of the Daily Telegraph's news about Pahang was about our previous operation - I think the Gurkhas and King's African Rifles got about eight - the rest was an operation near Lipis when the remainder of 6 Malay, acting on information, captured the 'Unity Press' - the Red propaganda show. Lau Fatt and Ha Yong were shot up by a Sten gun by one of their own men.

Lau Fatt had 30 bullets in him and still lived, his loyal bodyguard tried to escape with him, but they were caught the next day, and Lau Fatt died within 30 minutes. The ability of the Chinese to absorb Sten gun bullets is fantastic - they still run and live, though most eventually die through lack of medical aid.

The account of the Unity Press incident later given by a senior Special Branch officer is slightly different from that above. According to him, four Chinese State Committee members held a meeting, and while they slept that night one of their bodyguards tried to shoot all four (he then ran away and surrendered to the security forces). One was killed, Lau Fatt (who was in charge of the press) and another were wounded, and Hor Lung (called Ha Yong in my letter) escaped unharmed.[28] In 1958 Hor Lung, the commander of the MRLA in southern Malaya, surrendered and helped the security forces secure the capture or surrender of 150 terrorists for which he received large rewards.[29]

Their last doctors, two Japanese who'd been in the jungle since 1945, surrendered last year. Nine days nearly finishes me, but nine years on the run...!

At the end of the Second World War some Japanese soldiers refused to surrender and instead joined the MPAJA in order to continue fighting the British. When they realised that the MCP was not going to rebel immediately some of them headed for Siam to try to escape back home, some were caught by the British and some probably died in the jungle. The remainder lived with Chinese squatters. When it became difficult for a group of twenty to thirty in Perak to continue to be fed by their hosts they were murdered by the terrorists late in 1945. Chin Peng blames Lai Te and his British masters for ordering these killings, though if the British Army had known of the Japanese presence it would certainly have tried to capture them. The remaining thirty-five or so Japanese joined in the insurgency, some being killed, and some who had been identified by the British surrendered after their relations in Japan co-operated in writing leaflets or making recordings to be broadcast, urging them to give themselves up. The last two survivors returned to Japan from Siam in 1989, having spent forty-four years in the jungle, much of the time under appalling conditions, while being hunted by the security forces. Amazingly, they lived into their nineties![30]

2 JULY 1953, LIPIS

There are a few elephants near here, but not in the areas we've been searching in so far.

Despite the scarcity of elephants near Lipis, a staff officer at Brigade HQ, newly arrived from England, borrowed an elephant gun on his first weekend in Malaya, drove to a village a few miles away and asked the headman if there were any elephants about. The headman pointed to a clump of banana trees 100 yards away which were being ravaged by an elephant. It was duly shot, and one of its feet was stuffed and presented to the Brigade mess for use as a stool which we used to sit on when playing liar dice.

Tommy and Tony returned on Saturday. Food dumps (including four bottles of brandy), but no bandits.

10 JULY 1953, LIPIS

I expect I'll take some leave early next month, probably Fraser's Hill (quite safe - a recognised rest centre for us and for bandits who are thought to have rest camps there). My nickname ('Snow White') refers to my fair hair, no Malay has such colouring. After finding the food dump I was called 'Tuan QM' ('Sir Quartermaster') for a week or so.

About the name 'bandits'. I don't agree with it myself as to me they are armed, uniformed communists not at all different from those in Korea and Indo-China. Against this it's said that half of them don't know anything about Marxism, they are scattered and in small groups, and half of them are robbers such as have always existed in the jungle. I don't find this convincing. Some are robbers, but not many, all armies (including ours) have a rank and file unsure of what they're fighting for, and the fact that they are scattered makes them harder to kill. The real point, I think, is that calling them bandits and not the Malayan Races Liberation Army has a better effect on the population.

I have strong personal views on how to handle the population of Chinese who help them - and it's not a matter of names either! I'm convinced that no one could last the life of a bandit without some strong conviction, and this indicates a fairly thorough indoctrination by the leaders (who have no difficulty in getting replacements, witness 1948 5,000-6,000 bandits, 1953 5,000-6,000 bandits). The leaders are the key men; we have three with $75,000 (£9,000) on their heads within five miles of here.

Later estimates were 4,000-5,000 in 1948 and 5,500 in 1953, and though the later estimate for 1948 was 1,000 lower than the figure I quoted above, it confirms my claim that the terrorists had no difficulty in getting new recruits. Replacing leaders, however, remained a major problem for them throughout the Emergency.[31]

The military do not get any reward, though it's my ambition to catch a courier who carries 'subscriptions' from the Min Yuen to the bandits. It's an open secret that one got the other day had $10,000 (£1,166). The Police found the receipts, but the Army platoon got the cash, a highly satisfactory state of affairs. I have a rule in my platoon that I am to be the first to search dead or captured bandits and food stores - one can always hope for a courier! When captured, if anything is known against them (ie. murder) they are hanged, otherwise correction centres for minors, jail for adults. If they surrender they receive $500 (£60) plus rewards for information, and no punishment (unless they meet their own ex-friends when leading in a patrol - they tend to get killed by the bandits for surrendering). Re looting, the rule is 'all must be destroyed or handed in', but why give it to the Police who keep it themselves? My lighter was 'denied to the enemy' - I use it. Out on operations no one has tabs on you, and you use your own initiative, and I have no scruples with Red property - if we find it, it's ours!

Our company second in command (Captain Ibrahim bin Ismail MBE) came back from leave today - a nice fellow. He was an agent in Malaya during the war, landed by seaplane, and captured by the Japanese the first day. For a year he pretended to work for them relaying false information to the British on the wireless set. Actually he used a secret code indicating he was working under duress, and we knew all the time so kept asking for information about north Malaya and this misled the Japanese into thinking we would land there while we really landed in the south. He got the MBE for this.

On 31 October 1944 Ibrahim had flown by Catalina flying boat from Ceylon to the east coast of Malaya, and landed on the island of Pulau Perhentian Kecil.[32] After I left Malaya he rose to command 6 Malay in

1957, and eventually became General Tun Ibrahim bin Ismail, Chief of the Malaysian Armed Forces Staff. 'Tun' is a title awarded to very senior officers and statesmen and is the equivalent of 'Lord'. He has remained a good friend for fifty years, and insists I continue to call him 'Ib' despite his Malay lordship, his British knighthood and his two honorary PhDs. He enjoys pulling my leg because of the fact that he has two doctorates while I have only one, though I remind him that mine was earned while his were gifted.

He has led a charmed life as far as his military opponents are concerned. Not only did he escape execution by the Japanese when captured in 1944, but in 1974, during the second communist insurgency, the terrorists set up an assassination squad to kill senior security force officers. This squad made three attempts to kill Ibrahim while he drove through Kuala Lumpur between home and office. The first was aborted because a military police Land Rover happened by chance to be driving in front of his car; the second failed because a lorry happened to get between the ambush party and his car; the third was abandoned because two Chinese civilians standing close to the ambush site were (wrongly) identified by the terrorists as being detectives.[33]

He also had a narrow escape while on a jungle operation with me, but this time from 'friendly fire'. We were trudging along together near the head of my platoon immediately behind one of my men who was carrying a grenade-throwing rifle. On this gun's muzzle was screwed a metal cup which held a grenade with its safety pin removed but its firing arm held in by the sides of the cup. The grenade was retained in the cup by a muslin bag over its mouth, held on by a rubber band. In action the gun was fired by an uprated blank known as a balastite cartridge which blew the grenade through the muslin bag in an arc above the trees. The firing arm would spring off as the grenade left the cup, and the now armed grenade was intended to explode in front of fleeing terrorists to prevent their escape. The weapon was extremely dangerous to use in the jungle as there was a good chance that the grenade would strike a branch and drop back down on the heads of the patrol. In this incident, however, the man carrying the weapon tripped over a creeper and dropped the end of his rifle barrel so the grenade broke out through the muslin bag. Ibrahim and I got down behind a log while our men took shelter behind the trees. Fortunately, the seven-second fuse gave us ample time to get our heads down.

General Templer arrived in Lipis yesterday amid a crowd of armoured cars, escorts, planes overhead, etc. Doesn't mean to take any chances.

Templer's predecessor as High Commissioner, Sir Henry Gurney, was ambushed and killed in 1951 when his police escort proved totally inadequate – see the notes to my letter in Chapter 4 dated 9 December 1953.

19 JULY 1953, SUNGAI LIANG

Illustrations 10a and 10b in the picture section show 5 Platoon crossing a river, and number 15 shows the platoon's NCOs.

Came in from the operation last night, nothing seen or found. Weather was bad with heavy storms each night, howling wind, flashing lightning, thunder and buckets of rain. These storms get up in a few minutes. The first warning you get is an ever increasing moan as the wind increases, and you can rely on five minutes to get under cover. This sudden wind is most peculiar - no warning at all, just 'W O O S H!

Saw three very peculiar animals. The first was a spider, the most revolting looking thing. It had an olive green body the size of a hen's egg, and lots of hairy legs all placed in front of its head. When I decapitated it with a bayonet the legs continued to crawl towards me (minus body). I was nearly physically sick when I saw this.

There was absolutely no need to kill this creature which was probably a bird-eating spider, and was certainly not a man-eater!

The second was a millipede 10 inches long. Apparently the Sakai Aborigines eat them as a delicacy.

The use of the word 'Sakai' to describe Aborigines was criticised by the authorities in an early example of political correctness on the grounds that it had a pejorative sense of 'slave'. They insisted on 'Orang Asli' ('Native Man') instead, but everyone I knew continued to use the word 'Sakai', which was far more specific than 'Native Man', which was a description which could accurately be applied to many other races.

The third was a jungle fowl with a most peculiar cry. It consists of one note uttered every ten seconds at first, but slowly quickening up till it merges into the most blood-curdling laugh. Another thing I heard was what the boys call a riang-riang (a cicada) . It's a small insect which lives in a hole in the ground and exactly at 7.00 p.m. each night makes a noise like a very high note on a violin - very penetrating. At 7.00 p.m. bedlam breaks out in the jungle, frogs croaking, monkeys making human-like noises (you'd swear people were yelling at one another) riang-riang, jungle fowl, fireflies (pale green light, strong enough to read a small piece of paper by) float through the trees, leaves turn luminous, lightning flickers almost continuously. At first the whole performance is quite frightening, but you hardly notice it after a time.

24 JULY 1953, LIPIS

I have a slightly ulcerated foot so hope not to have to go in till after my leave. Am enclosing the imprint of a bandit propaganda stamp found in a food store. It's a hand carved block of mahogany with a raised five pointed star and depressed hammer and sickle. Some ardent Red must have spent quite a lot of time carving that and thinking of the Utopia to come. I know the sort of Utopia we have in mind for him!

The stamp, which was stained dark red by the ink in which it had been dipped to produce coloured imprints, was probably not used for propaganda purposes but to authenticate MCP letters demanding money from Chinese merchants. Illustrations 8 and 9 in the picture section show the stamp and imprint. A similar stamp had earlier been found in Selangor and had been used by a police officer to fake some MCP documents which deceived a terrorist who was in charge of one of their arms dumps into revealing its location.[34]

I saw a silk sheet with paintings of soldiers and Chinese lettering on it the other day - used by the Reds as a backcloth to pep lectures given to the rank and file by the leaders in their jungle camps.

4 AUGUST 1953, KAMPONG JERKOH/SUNGAI CHENN'A

I'm still out on operations stuck on a little river in the jungle. We've now been out nine days and have at least a couple more to do. Our job is patrolling the river, very little work in fact. This operation has been quite interesting as we have three surrendered bandits with us and four Iban (Dyak) trackers from Borneo.

We have covered a lot of ground, found several old camps, and I found another food dump, not so good as the last as it was nearly empty.

One of the bandits was the bodyguard who turned traitor and shot Lau Fat and another big bandit last month, and then surrendered. He's a nasty little character, a killer if ever there was one. He clings to us like a leech as he's very afraid of being recaptured. The other two are solely to keep him company, he's a shade afraid of our boys too!

We were always surprised that surrendered terrorists were so willing to betray their ex-comrades. Various explanations for this have been advanced, but none made much sense to me except revenge for bad treatment by superiors.[35]

The Ibans are charming characters, tattooed from tip to toe and with gold teeth with red and blue centres, big hits with the Iban ladies from all accounts!

All young Ibans had their natural teeth removed as soon as they could afford to buy gold replacements which were fitted as false teeth.

They all carry the most fearsome-looking knives decorated with tufts of human hair. One does not enquire too closely the source of this hair, but tacitly assume it's Japanese. They are fascinated by my fair hair, but I've made it quite clear that mine is solely to decorate my head, and I'm very attached to it. An offer to tattoo me was also firmly refused.

Their leader speaks very quaint English, and I spend most evenings sitting in their tent chatting with him. He badly wants to go to England, and his favourite question is: 'How much one nice English baby?' At first I was simple enough to assume he meant how much to raise an infant, further elucidation indicated the baby in question was considerably older! ('One nice Iban baby $10 - you want go Borneo?!') Their expressions when we had a sick man evacuated by helicopter were killingly funny. They'd never seen a helicopter before, and to see one land in a clearing, pick up one of our boys, and then go straight up and disappear was almost too much for them.

We had two boys sick, both with temperatures of 102. One was unable to walk, and I had to carry him to the clearing, a hell of a weight he was too. It's very worrying when they get ill and delirious. The helicopter is a great blessing, but cutting a clearing big enough (30 yards) is difficult in thick jungle. The other was able to stagger the three miles to the road, but looked very sick. My first aid consists of a stiff rum and two aspirin. I also administer these to myself as a bracer in case the patient dies. I feel so sorry for them as they're only kids and look very pathetic.

Although each platoon had a medicine pack I had received no guidance on how to treat the sick. I had no confidence in our medical orderly because when I once asked him to pull out a splinter of bamboo from my hand, he fainted. Looking back, I think he was probably terrified at having been asked to treat an English officer for the first time, and that I should have tried to build up his confidence instead of ignoring him from then on.

We've had two airdrops, and on one we got pineapples, coconuts, rum and cigarettes, all very welcome. At the moment we are camped near a Malay village. I am a source of great interest to the kids some of whom have never seen a white man before.

Some of the children had also never heard a radio before, so when we tuned in our wireless to music on Radio Malaya and put headphones on them the expressions on their faces were a delight to see.

I get coconuts, eggs and chickens from them which is an improvement on bully beef. The river is quite nice to bathe in, but is unfortunately inhabited by lintah - a huge leech nine inches long (before feeding). He takes a lot of blood and leaves a nasty hole. The boys are terrified of them, and stampeded for the bank when one started on my foot (so did I, only faster!).

One of our other companies a few miles to the north was ambushed yesterday - their Iban tracker was killed, and two men wounded. They killed one bandit, and captured another. Our Ibans were very upset about their friend's death, and fingered their knives suggestively. The three bandits retired to my tent promptly with their guns. I retired to the smallest room in the jungle to let things cool off!

The Ibans wanted terrorist heads as souvenirs to take home with them to Borneo to continue their tradition of head-hunting. On the few occasions we had them with us we did not find them to be much use at tracking (which was probably our fault), and their main value to us was in retrieving parachutes carrying airdropped supplies which had lodged in the branches of tall trees – their climbing skills were incredible. I once watched an Iban walk out from the trunk of a tree along a branch about 150ft above the ground to cut the cords holding a trapped container of food.

> Our battalion commander is Lieutenant-Colonel Laugher, pronounced 'Law' unless you want to be extra orderly officer. An OBE and MC - extremely rude, very keen, nicknamed 'Skinny', rumour has it that this is because he's a mean bastard. I wouldn't know.

I had not yet seen much of the Colonel, which is why I repeated the rumour which I had heard at Port Dickson that he was a mean bastard. This turned out to be totally untrue. I did not learn the true explanation of his nickname of 'Skinny' until 1999, when I read a book by an officer who had served in the Dorsetshire Regiment in India in 1934.[36] The Colonel had then been a subaltern in the Dorsets, and the author described him as 'Skinny Laugher, very fat'. The nickname was thus one of those which provided an opposite description of the actual appearance of the subject – like 'Tiny' as a nickname for a man such as Major-General 'Tiny' Barber, who was about 6ft 6in tall.[37] By the time I met the Colonel he was certainly not fat.

> I think the Korean truce will have a favourable result out here. Thousands of leaflets were dropped telling the Reds of this truce, but it will be ages before all of them know. Their leaders suppress the leaflets.
>
> A bandit committee member surrendered yesterday and says a number of bandits want to do so, but are scared, of their own side, and of us. The area of our last operation is being bombed today, and shot up with rockets. Probably will kill several million ants and no bandits, but will scare them plenty.
>
> This time last year I was on my way to Aldershot - who'd have thought then....!

Notes

1 Newman, p.305; *Annual Abstract*, 2004, p.261.
2 Miers, p.94.
3 Short, p.349.
4 Royle, p.174.
5 Miller, *Menace*, p.15.
6 Short, p.350.
7 Chin Peng, pp.311-313.
8 Holman, p.139.
9 Toye, p.v, Chapter VII, pp.166-172; Bose, p.294.

10 16 January 1992. A copy of this obituary also appears in *The Daily Telegraph Second Book of Obituaries, Heroes and Adventurers* (1996), pp.223-26, where the description 'A legendary character' has inexplicably been changed to 'A noted character'. However, the caption of the photograph of the Colonel which accompanied his obituary in the newspaper also included the word 'legendary'.
11 Chin Peng, p.289.
12 Miller, *Jungle*, pp.39-40.
13 Information supplied by Tony Froom.
14 Carew, p.142.
15 Middlebrook, p.17.
16 Chin Peng, p.321.
17 Farwell, p.268, says that the corporal was left behind in Burma, but this should have read Malaya; Neillands, *A Fighting Retreat*, p.217.
18 Postgate, p.179.
19 Short, pp.418, 422.
20 Chin Peng, p.404.
21 Spencer Chapman, *The Jungle*, p.354.
22 Jackson, p.20.
23 Miller, *Menace*, p.15.
24 Chin Peng, p.278.
25 Short, p.342.
26 Robinson, p.90.
27 R. Thompson, p.48.
28 A. Chin, p.37.
29 Chin Peng, p.401.
30 Ibid., pp.145-48.
31 R. Thompson, p.47 (1948); Short, p.349 (1953). Estimates of the number of terrorists vary considerably, but Thompson's and Short's figures seem to be the most reliable. Chin Peng (p.398) admits that he never knew how many were ever in the MRLA.
32 Ibrahim bin Ismail, p.68.
33 A. Chin, pp.236-37.
34 Miller, *Menace*, p.92.
35 Short, p.364, footnote 25.
36 Mains, p.31.
37 J. Thompson, pp.242-43.

CHAPTER 4

Jungle Operations, Illness and Leave: 11 August–19 December 1953

11 AUGUST 1953, COLISEUM HOTEL, KUALA LUMPUR, ON SIX DAYS' LEAVE

This small Chinese hotel, in which Simon Pritchard and I lunched in 2003 during our visit to our regiment after fifty years, was very popular with planters during the Emergency, and at lunchtime the table in the bar used to be stacked high with their guns. The speciality of the restaurant has always been a steak cooked on a red-hot iron slab placed in front of the diners. The hotel was also popular with Lai Te, who used to stay there during the war, and this raises questions about the political sympathies of the management during the Emergency. If they were MCP supporters, the lunchtime chatter of the planters would have supplied much information to the terrorists.[1]

Arrived yesterday after the 100 mile drive with the convoy - over the worst road I've ever seen - twists and winds at 7,000 feet, and as wide as a country lane. The views are magnificent, jungle-clad mountains stretching into the distance, green at first and then blue and grey.

Major Rosslyn has returned; first impressions, madly keen, still not fit, no conversation except on army matters, and a hell of a strain to have around.

First impressions were accurate; nobody could stand him.

My moustache apparently makes me look about 35, and a subaltern in the Lancers which were escorting the convoy mistook me for a major yesterday, saluted and 'Sir'ed me for about ten minutes until he spotted his mistake (Malay Regiment pips look like a major's crown at first glance). I loved every minute of it, and he was furious when he found out!

On operations my pack with four day's rations with clothes and equipment weighs 70 lbs. A lot to pull up hills of one in four and jungle covered.

We sometimes carried five days' rations, and when later I read a book by a major in the Royal Marine Commandos in which he said that in Malaya his men carried only three days' rations because to carry more tired them too much I think this showed the effect of jungle conditions on British men.[2] My 70lb pack was exactly half my body weight of ten stone.

17 AUGUST 1953, BRITISH MILITARY HOSPITAL, KUALA LUMPUR

This, and the following letter, were carefully worded to limit my parents' concerns. The editorial notes convey a rather more accurate picture of events.

After I got back to Lipis I didn't feel too good - a touch of dysentery and whatnot so they decided a spell in hospital would bring the colour back to the old cheeks. They got me in by helicopter, 45 minutes from Raub. Lovely journey, and I'm sorry I couldn't appreciate much of it as I was pretty dozy.

The stretcher was attached to the outside of the helicopter so was exposed to the down draught of the rotor blades, but fortunately I soon passed out. When we landed the waiting medical orderlies, who had been told nothing about my condition, lifted me off the stretcher by my legs which were covered in jungle ulcers. Ouch!

I'm looked after very well here, and am feeling my old self again. Don't know how long I shall be here, until some jungle ulcers on my leg heal up I expect. Apparently very high temperatures are not uncommon out here (mine was 104).

Malaria was the usual cause of very high temperatures. When suffering from this fever, Pat Noone and Spencer Chapman apparently had temperatures of 106 and 105.5 respectively.[3]

23 AUGUST 1953, BRITISH MILITARY HOSPITAL, KUALA LUMPUR

I leave here tomorrow feeling completely OK. General Templer came round the hospital yesterday, and I had a few words with his eminence - usual stuff, name, regiment, etc.

I don't think the general liked me. After the introductory formalities he asked how I was feeling. 'Much better, thank you Sir.' He turned to the accompanying matron. 'See this officer is returned to his unit tomorrow,' he said, and moved on to the next bed. Although my ulcers had not healed, I was discharged two days later. An armoured scout car was sent from the battalion to collect me, but bored by the slow haul up the Gap Road over the mountains I took over the driving and soon rammed a large milestone because the view through the narrow slit in the armoured front was very restricted. The scout car did not seem to go so well after that, and when I arrived back at base our furious transport officer told me the repairs would cost a small fortune; I suggested he sent the bill to General Templer. When a book about the Emergency was published in 1971 I was delighted to learn that Templer visited hospitals as part of his programme of 'winning the hearts and minds of the people'.[4]

According to his official biographer, Templer had long had a record of unsympathetic treatment of the military sick. In 1918, when a subaltern in France, he had been evacuated to the rear with diphtheria. He found himself lying on a stretcher next to an officer who was close to death, and who was labelled to be sent to the American Ladies' Hospital. Templer, who was labelled to be sent to a far less comfortable field hospital, switched labels. In 1941, after his ADC had been badly wounded in a leg, Templer asked him how long he would be on crutches. The ADC said he had been told about a week. 'Make it five days', said Templer, who later kicked away the man's stick saying: 'Look, you can stand quite well without one.' His own medical problems, however, required rather different treatment. In 1944, when he injured his back in Italy, he sent his then ADC to walk through a minefield to fetch a cottage door to which he could be strapped.[5]

28 AUGUST 1953, LIPIS

The Colonel, who has just paid a visit here, was in a sunny mood (for once) and insisted that I take a week's leave.

Only once did he ever refuse me leave. I had received an invitation from the University of London to attend a graduation ceremony, and as a joke I asked the Colonel for leave so that I might accept. He asked how long I wanted, and nearly had a fit when I said only six weeks for a troopship home, plus a day for the ceremony, plus six weeks for a troopship back.

1 SEPTEMBER 1953, FRASER'S HILL, ON A WEEK'S LEAVE

Over the weekend news of a possible ambush came in, and one section of my platoon was told to do it. The colonel wouldn't let me go in until I'd had a week's leave so Tommy led them. The bandits came OK, but caught our ambush changing positions, and although shots were exchanged, no one was killed. I was furious as I'd told the colonel I could go on leave afterwards, but he wouldn't let me go in. The bandits were within eight yards of Tommy, who missed them with his machine gun - clot. They were a party led by a Chinese woman named Ah Wong. She carries a Tommy gun, and is a hot poppet.

The other two big noises in north Pahang are Osman China (a Malay bandit leader who has already survived many ambushes, and is supposed to bear a charmed life) and an Indian called Vincent; both have big prices on their heads.

Osman China was actually a Chinese man who had been adopted as a child by a Malay family. He spent his time trying to convert Malays to communism, and claimed to have survived seven ambushes. He surrendered in December 1954 and earned $60,000 (£7,500) by helping the security forces.[6] I have been unable to find out anything about 'Vincent' and wonder whether my information about this man was long out of date. Perhaps he was the leader of the Indian communists called Veerasenan who had joined the terrorists but had been shot dead in 1949.[7] In 1953 there were very few Indian terrorists, none of whom could be called 'big noises'.

As regards charmed lives, one Malay bandit leader said: 'Only a silver bullet will kill me', and survived numerous attempts until finally a shotgun made a hole in him. The subaltern who got him got an awful rocket from His Excellency for parading this character through the Chinese villages with a notice saying: 'What price silver bullets?' The sight of a dead bandit in a lorry is supposed to be too upsetting to the populace. Personally I should have had him embalmed, and

present at village council meetings as a salutary reminder that banditry doesn't pay.

Templer's concern for Chinese sensitivities was matched by our idiotic Foreign Office, who insisted that communist China, whose government we had recognised in 1950, should be allowed to appoint consuls in Malayan towns, despite being warned that these officials would help the terrorists. Did our Foreign Office not know that Chinese communists had been terrorising Malaya for two years? Only the threat of resignation by the then High Commissioner caused this stupid instruction to be withdrawn.[8]

In my letter of 1 September I forecast certain coming events based on the information available to me at the time. These are shown below with notes of what actually happened to demonstrate how difficult it is for soldiers to forecast their future movements:

FORECAST	ACTUALITY
Our operations will continue until January	Operations continued until April
We retrain in February and March in Penang	We retrained in May and June in Temerloh
We will move in April to Kedah	We remained in Pahang
Troopship home in June	Plane home in August

9 SEPTEMBER 1953, LIPIS

In the middle of two weeks retraining - very strenuous. Am not sure how long I will be able to stand Rosslyn. Don't want to apply for a transfer, but will consider it if he fails to get his course in England which means he would leave before Xmas if he gets it. He's missed his profession, he should have been a preacher or a private detective, he's an incredible talker, never stops and all one subject - the Army. Ib, Tony and I have constant arguments with him over his treatment of men (to no avail) and none of us is very happy here at the moment. Anyway, I rather enjoy the rows as not being a regular I can, and do, say what I think, and it's often pretty hot!

On my first night back in the mess after one long and tiring operation I was woken by Rosslyn some time after midnight because he wanted to discuss a brilliant idea he had just had for how we could in future carry six days' rations instead of five. I was later told my language had not been that of an officer and a gentleman.

17 SEPTEMBER 1953, LIPIS

We go out tomorrow by helicopter, destination unknown, after 30 bandits, another wild goose chase I expect. Taking five days rations, but may get an airdrop.

27 SEPTEMBER 1953, KAMPONG BELITIK

At present am on the tenth day of the operation with at least another three to go, and possibly more. We went in by helicopter - quite an experience, 60 men and three helicopters, four men in each plane.

The helicopters' poor lifting power limited the number of troops each could carry to four at a time. Thus, five trips per helicopter were needed for three helicopters to lift sixty men. The continuing noise could be heard for miles around and warned every terrorist in the vicinity about what was going on.

There is no door, and you sit and look into space on either side - quite disturbing! Each helicopter trails a 15 foot rope, and if the ground is rough it hovers while you climb down the rope; if smooth it lands, and you walk out. Luckily it was smooth!

We landed in a deserted village about ten miles in the jungle, and split up into platoons. Everyone except me seems to have bumped bandits - Ib got one, and Tony wounded one. All I found were two deserted camps, each for 50 bandits, one of them complete with trenches, log sentry posts and an alarm system of rattles, a cookhouse with six ovens and a parade ground. This camp had contained Malay bandits (90 per cent of all bandits are Chinese) as we found a sentry roster with Malay names on it. The bandits have given up defending these camps, and always run when we attack, just as well for us! Tony met 24, and they all ran, one leaving his shoes behind he was in such a hurry.

This is the worst operation so far for discomfort. The ground is a maze of rivers and hills making map reading impossible, and to cap it all it's the wet season - torrential rain and thunderstorms, and everything soaking wet. All clothes perpetually soaking, and quite cold, especially early morning. I have a tot of rum before going to bed, and nips during the night.

In a lighter vein the operation has been quite interesting as regards animals. I killed a large green snake by cutting off its head, and when one of my men touched the severed head with a stick five minutes later it snapped and bit the stick - you never can be too careful.

Another unnecessary act of slaughter. The snake was coiled on top of a bush sleeping peacefully in a shaft of sunlight which was slanting through a gap in the tree canopy. It was no danger to anyone until I cut off its head.

We also found the first tortoise I've seen since I've been out here, two foot long and very heavy. My men wanted to eat him, but much to their disgust I wouldn't let them. He would not have anything to do with me, and stayed in his shell in spite of offers of food.

A rare example of mercy, but when later that day my men caught a tiny deer about a foot long, I assumed they would keep it as a pet, but that evening when I enquired after its health, I was presented with a mess tin filled with a pile of rice with a small slice of venison on top.

It's the best time of year for jungle fruits, several types are quite edible and one (rambutan, 'hairy shell') is quite nice, sharp and juicy. I had tea one day off a jungle fowl's egg; bigger than a hen's egg and with the same taste.

All these little things make operations interesting (we've heard three tigers during this operation) but 99 per cent of the time is sheer discomfort and hard work with the mental worry of never knowing to within 1,000 yards where you are. Until the Emergency no one ever went in the jungle in Malaya, and the maps (printed circa 1927) are sketchy and inaccurate (who wants an accurate map of a useless area?).

Wrong. Pre-war surveyors, loggers, naturalists and anthropologists went into parts of the jungle as well as native hunters and fruit gatherers. The maps we used for jungle navigation were drawn to a scale of 1in to the mile. They showed rivers and streams, estates and cultivations, roads and a few tracks, lakes and swamps, towns and villages, contours every 50ft and the height of prominent hills. They looked extremely detailed and professional, but were not nearly as accurate as they first appeared. When we arrived at a river which I was sure I had identified on the map but found it was flowing in the opposite direction to that shown, I faced the question: 'Was the surveyor wrong or am I?' We could never understand how the surveys could have been made to show such detail as appeared on the maps, as visibility was so limited that plotting the position of small features such as streams, or correctly positioning contours, would have necessitated visits to every bit of ground, and in the 14,000 square miles of Pahang this would have been impossible.

No river is larger than the River Pinn, and 90 per cent of them are smaller. Imagine trying to place hundreds of little trickles on an inaccurate map!

The River Pinn is a stream which ran behind my aunt's house at Pinner in Middlesex. The map on page 113 shows a typical number of streams and rivers in quite a small area of jungle. In his book *The Jungle is Neutral*, Spencer Chapman described the difficulties of map-reading in Pahang:

> I was now to learn that navigation in thick mountainous jungle is the most difficult in the world – and I had always rather fancied myself at map-reading and finding my way in all types of country from Greenland to Australia. In the first place, it is quite impossible to find out where you are on the map. The limit of your visibility is fifty to a hundred yards, and even if you are on some steep hillside, where a small landslide has opened up a window through which you can catch a glimpse of another steep blue tree-clad hillside, you are none the wiser as one hill is exactly like another. There are no landmarks – and if there were you could not see them. Another difficulty is that there is no way of judging distance: it took us more than a week to realise we were taking eight hours to travel one mile on the map instead of the three or four miles we imagined, judging by the amount of time we were spending. Perhaps the greatest impediment to navigation is that, having decided to move in a certain direction, you are quite unable to do so owing to the difficulties of the terrain. We were continually forced off our course by swamps, thickets, precipices, outcrops of rock, and rivers. It was impossible even to follow a ridge unless it was very steep and clearly marked. With such limited visibility it was seldom clear which was the main ridge, and we soon found ourselves down in the valley bottom, having inadvertently followed a subsidiary spur.[9]

Other navigational problems resulted from the inaccuracy of the maps, and the absence of any maps of certain parts of Pahang.

There's no danger in being lost as a compass bearing will always bring you to a road, but one must know the map reference in order to receive an airdrop of food (two so far).

A sound way of escaping from the jungle *without* a compass or a map is to follow a stream downhill. It will meet a bigger stream, and then a river which will eventually lead to a village on its bank. The only problem is if the stream being followed disappears into a swamp which must then be crossed or circled round to find a stream flowing out.

29 September. At present trying to get in contact with the others - our wireless has broken down (can receive, but cannot send). This operation has produced four surrenders so far, and we have a plane constantly circling overhead broadcasting messages from the surrendered bandits in Chinese. 'Come in chaps, good treatment', etc. We get sick of the sound of it (Chinese is a weird language). Plenty of monkeys swinging through the trees at a fine speed and making almost human-like calls. Four large tortoises were found in the last bandit camp so evidently the bandits like them for food as our boys do.

One morning during this operation, believing we were near a terrorist camp, I was leading a section, creeping forward through the undergrowth on hands and knees when a huge hairy blue caterpillar crawled across the ground under my nose. I had never seen one like it before, and longed to stop to put it in one of my pouches. Then I bumped into a large hump of rock sticking out of the ground which was glistening all over with gold-coloured flakes. There was certainly gold not far away as there was a mine in the Tersang Forest Reserve about fourteen miles to the south-west of Ulu Penjom, where the rock was situated. When we had finished searching for the camp (which wasn't there) I went back to try to find the caterpillar (new to science?) and the rock (encrusted with iron pyrites or with gold?), but failed to find either. Had I been luckier, I might have become a millionaire with a new species of moth named after me.

2 OCTOBER 1953, LIPIS

The operation came to a sudden end when rations for 100 men were dropped to the wrong company, and we were left without. Made a long dash for the road last night, and got back to camp filthy, wet, and tired. Out again tomorrow (another 14 days? Hell!). Some of your letters were dropped in on one of our airdrops, always looked for and very welcome. Towards the end of the operation we linked up with a platoon of ex-bandits now part of the security forces and led by a British Police Officer who has a personal bodyguard of five men in case the ex-Reds change their minds again. What a set-up! Just typical of this war, and indicative of how little you can trust the Chinese in spite of General Templer's boosting of these platoons. The ex-bandits have not been told of the bodyguard - they think the five are just to make up the numbers.

Twelve such ex-terrorist platoons called the Special Operational Volunteer Force were set up in the summer of 1953.[10]

On the last day of the operation I saw my first scorpion, blue-green and nine inches long, and very keen to sting my rifle when prodded. We also had a panic when we found the biggest snake so far, between six and seven feet long. We were crossing a river, and it was taking a bath - most unfortunate!

The snake was quite thick, and dirty white in colour. During our confrontation it reared up the high slippery muddy bank to try to get out of the river, and this enabled me to estimate its length.

The platoon took to the trees, leaving me standing on a log in the middle swiping at it with a parang - couldn't see a man for miles, just me and the snake. The Battle of Sungai Lalang - the enemy was driven off!

Our publicity officer is no bloody good, and never insists on the Malay Regiment being named in the news although the six battalions have between them killed 400 bandits. The Ghurkas seem to be the glamour boys for news.

I have been unable to obtain any official figures of the number of terrorists killed by the Malay Regiment between 1948 and 1953, though I believe it was probably much more than 400. The regiment's battalions formed about a quarter of all the infantry battalions operating during those years, and during that time 4,833 terrorists were killed by the security forces, but I have been unable to find what proportion of this total had been killed by the Army.[11]

When Lieutenant-Colonel Laugher died, his obituary in the *Daily Telegraph* stated that: 'from 1953 to 1956, under his command, the 6th Battalion of the

Malay Regiment killed more bandits than any other battalion'.[12]

Why he was awarded only a mention in despatches instead of a DSO for the results he achieved remains a mystery to me.

Sorry about the writing, but my fingers are cut about a bit and writing is painful.

8 OCTOBER 1953, SUNGAI KERUPAN/SUNGAI KETIR

After the long operation we went out again on an abortive ambush for two days. Last night we went to a party at the British Adviser's house. Met the Sultan of Pahang and his new wife (number two).

9 OCTOBER 1953, LIPIS

I shall probably be going out again on another operation tomorrow on some hot information (all information is 'hot', and one gets cynical after a time). Down river by boat, I think, better than walking!

LATER Go out tomorrow 2.30 a.m. for three days. If the information is correct we should kill some as we know where 14 bandits are camped, and I've been chosen (lucky old me!) to sort them out with my platoon. I doubt if they'll all be there, and we shall be taking three machine guns, two grenade-throwing rifles and other little surprises. Probably a false alarm like 90 per cent of operations, but I have hopes this time.

12 OCTOBER 1953, SUNGAI MATOK

The most colossal mess-up of an operation ever. I was shown by the police a 'Top Secret' letter containing the statement made by an informer. It ran something like this:

'Whilst going from Lipis to Kampong Kenong by boat on 7 October I saw two Malays dressed in khaki carrying food near the mouth of the Sungai Matok. I landed from my boat as it was unusual to see Malays in this area, and I was suspicious. I followed them for an hour till they came to two houses, and were met by 14 bandits. I then ran.'

The maps showed no houses in the area which was marked on the map as primary jungle, and the Police knew of no Malays there. As Saturday was a Red Celebration it was thought that the food was for a party to be held for 15 or so bandits known to be in the area. The plan was that I should meet four boats at Lipis at 2.30 a.m. on Saturday, and be briefed finally by a police officer. I had not been down the river before.

The policeman did not turn up, and it was not until 4.30 a.m. that I found the boats (owner asleep, and not yet briefed). I held a brief Orders Group by the light of a candle, and had to decide whether to postpone the operation as it takes three hours to get there, and it gets light at 6.30 a.m., and we mustn't be seen. I decided to go - not I'm afraid because of any rational reason, but because I was so furious I couldn't trust myself to go back and be polite to everyone concerned! We poled down river, and landed at 6.45 a.m. I approached the area by a roundabout route, and was in position by 10.00 a.m. There were six houses in all, not agreeing with the information.

I took two men with me, and went forward to recce. We spent a long time on each of the first four houses, all were deserted. At the fifth we heard the noise of cutting in the jungle. We took half an hour to crawl 20 yards through the undergrowth, and found a Malay dressed in khaki cutting atap (palm thatch used to make houses). Due to our extreme care I got within five feet of him without being detected, took aim at his heart with my carbine, and took the first pressure on the trigger. My two men did exactly the same.

Something stopped me killing him; I didn't fire, something was fishy. If he was a bandit, why no sentry? And where was his weapon? I took a chance, and stepped out of cover and stuck my carbine in his ribs - he nearly fainted with fright. When he recovered he pleaded with us not to kill him, claimed he was a rice planter, a Kampong (village) Guard (ie. a member of the security forces), and had a family in the nearby house. We made him lead us to it, questioned him, inspected his identity card, paraded his family (two wives, a mother and two kids) and sent for the other family in the other house (eight people, thus 8 plus 6 equals the 14 'bandits' of our information). All was quite in order. He and the other man had been down to the river on the 7th to buy fish. However, they had been dressed in Kampong Guard uniform and carrying shotguns - a fact not mentioned by our informer. No bandits were in the area (the banana trees were loaded with ripe fruit, a sure sign of the absence of bandits).

All there was were two peaceful Malay families living in the jungle, and the breadwinner within an inch of being killed by yours truly. If I had, no blame would have been attached to me as I would have been more than justified on the information I had been given. I won't go into the apologies of the Police, who were very thankful I didn't shoot. What was the explanation? A number of possible causes. First, the informer. He may have been activated by hate for the rice planters; personal feuds and giving information to shop your enemy has been known before. He may have made a genuine mistake, although there is no excuse for not mentioning the Kampong Guard uniforms. He may just have hoped we met some bandits by coincidence, he would still have got his reward (many cases of this, no real information, just wishful thinking on the part of the informer). Secondly, bone bloody idleness on the part of the Police in not knowing of the existence of the Malays in the area - they'd been there since 1926! I'm afraid my comments on my return were more lurid than helpful. The next information the Police give me will have to be so hot before I go out it won't be true!

It was disgraceful that the local police did not know of the presence of two Malay Kampong Guards living at the site of the supposed terrorist camp – after all they were supposed to be responsible for selecting, arming and training these guards! Their informant was almost certainly a liar. To call the fourteen Malays 'bandits' when at least two of them were children was ridiculous.

Enclosed some Japanese 'banana' money, a relic of the wartime occupation I found in one of the deserted houses.

An old suitcase in one of these houses was filled with these bank notes which were named after the picture of banana trees which was printed on the front. When the British returned in 1945 the currency was declared valueless, a move which Chin Peng criticises for destroying the savings of the labourers and reducing them to penury.[13] According to others, however, the

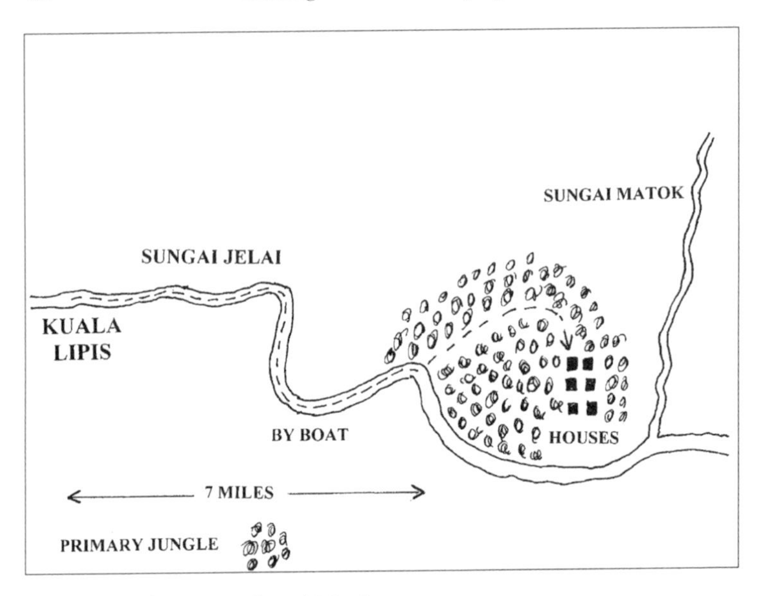

Sketch map of Operation Sungai Matok.

Japanese 'uncontrolled issue of paper-money created a worthless currency' so the labourers' savings in banana money would already have lost all their value by the time the British returned.[14]

14 OCTOBER 1953, LIPIS

I pride myself on my sense of direction, but 20 yards in the jungle and I'm lost. A compass is the only answer, it rarely leaves your hand.

No chance of a second pip. Under Army Regulations must do two years as a 2nd Lieutenant. I shall have done eighteen months on release.

17 OCTOBER 1953, LIPIS

We are going out again tomorrow morning at 4.00 a.m. after four cultivations which have been spotted from the air, all within 4,000 yards of Lipis! Nearest 1,000 yards - cheeky blighters.

22 OCTOBER 1953, SUNGAI KERUPAN/SUNGAI KETIR

Returned from a four day operation last night. Nothing found, and the worst country I've been in so far - belukar (a secondary jungle and scrub with grass and bushes ten feet high and no shelter from the sun). Our wireless set broke down, the map proved wrong, and we set a whole valley on fire by accident. Now I know how terrible a bush fire must be, the heat is unbearable and it spreads rapidly. And as a last straw we failed to get our airdrop of food. Half a coconut was all the food I had yesterday until 9.00 p.m. last night when we staggered out of the bush more dead than alive. I could hear the sweat dripping off my arms and body onto the dead leaves as we marched.

We had lit a fire to mark our position for a plane which was trying to find us to make a parachute drop of food, and we used a smoke grenade to increase the smoke from the fire. When the grenade exploded, burning phosphorous shot out onto the surrounding dry grass, and set it alight. Before we could beat it out it spread, and soon became so hot we could not get near it. A breeze began to drive the flames up the valley, and when I looked at my map I was horrified to see a Malay village marked at the head of the valley. I had visions of screaming children, and ordered a patrol to follow the blaze, and when they got near the village to fire their rifles to warn the villagers. Fortunately the patrol returned with the good news that the village had long since been abandoned. Several weeks later I was bought drinks by some RAF pilots who had heard that I had started the fire which had blackened the whole valley and made it a valuable aid to their navigation.

Am looking forward to receiving my birthday parcels. Last birthday I was on seven charges at Eaton Hall. If I have to spend this one in the jungle it will be the last straw!

On 18 November 1952, my 22nd birthday, I was charged with idleness on parade by a Major Catto, a company commander at Eaton Hall, for moving my hand to check I still had my bayonet which a cadet behind me had whispered was missing. As a result I spent every evening for a week parading in Field Service Marching Order being inspected by the orderly officer – an experience I came to loathe. In September 1953 the Colonel told me to take a newly joined company commander with me on my next operation, to give him some jungle experience and help his acclimatisation. When I met this officer I recognised Major Catto, but he did not recognise me. We started our first day's march at dawn, and I chose a route which went up every hill and through every swamp in the area, and allowed no halts till dark. 'Revenge is sweet,' saith the Lord! I was pretty tired myself by the time we stopped, and Major Catto seemed close to death. As we lay in our tent that night drinking medicinal rum, he said sadly that he did not think he could cope with the jungle, and was contemplating early retirement. I decided we were now all square, so I told him why I'd made his day a misery, and convinced him that he would be able to cope with more 'normal' marches. Being a perfect gentleman he forgave me, and we got on well thereafter. I am glad that we did, as I now don't think I should have treated him so badly. After all, I had been guilty of making a mistake on parade, and though I had been conned into doing so by a leg-pulling comrade, Major Catto had not known about this at the time.

> **Off again tomorrow morning, short operation (three days) I hope. Same area unfortunately, it's bloody. Just finished reading 'Jungle Green'. Substantially correct though he lays it on a bit thick. I must say I didn't find the jungle all that terrifying and the noises have never yet kept me awake. I sleep eleven hours and still feel dog tired!**

This book by Major Arthur Campbell MC, who commanded a company of the Suffolk Regiment during the early years of the Emergency, was published in July 1953. Though popular with the British public it was disliked by the Malayan Chinese for its criticisms of their support for the terrorists. It contains both descriptions of the author's personal experiences and the experiences of other officers, but unfortunately without identifying which were his and which were not. My comment that he lays it on a bit thick refers to his somewhat exaggerated accounts of the unpleasantness of conditions in the jungle and the difficulties of moving through it. The principal theme of the book is the search for, and eventual killing in 1952, of Liew Kon Kim, the commander of the terrorists' 4th Independent Company.[15] Chin Peng described Liew as being 'one of our most successful guerilla leaders', and criticises the British for parading his corpse in a lorry around new villages for three days although Campbell makes no mention of this in his book.[16]

25 OCTOBER 1953, SUNGAI KERUPAN/SUNGAI KETIR

> **My Malay is fairly good now though I can't spell half the words I use. This doesn't matter as I never have to write it. I'm much stronger on the coarser type of Malay than on**

Rajah Malay. Mine is definitely Bazaar Malay, and much more useful.

Spencer Chapman on Malay/Japanese co-operation is not too reliable. He lived only with Chinese who hate Malays' guts and would lose no opportunity of blackening their reputations. According to my boys the Chinese did all the co-operating. The answer is that both did, and who can blame them? The Japanese didn't change the way of life of the peasants much, only the educated and independent minority. As long as you got your rice why worry who is governing?

I was quite wrong in saying that the Japanese did not change the way of life of the peasants much because in fact they massacred very many poor Chinese. Japan had long been at war with China and the two races hated each other. The Chinese and Malays in Malaya also did not like each other, and after independence in 1957 I was surprised that this did not result in frequent conflict between the two races whose populations were of roughly similar size. There were serious riots between the two races in Kuala Lumpur in 1969, and my friend General Ibrahim played a major role in bringing them to an end. Peace appears to have reigned ever since.

Came in yesterday from a two day operation - abortive. In the swamps this time, how I love leeches! They don't trouble me so much now, my blood must have thinned. Many amusing sights for the men. Tuan up to his neck in oily black water. Tuan falling off slippery logs on his back in the swamp. Tuan completely submerged for minutes on end while they prodded for me with sticks. Tuan giving a helping hand up a bank to his batman, overbalancing, and falling in himself. Tuan's fluent language on all these occasions.

When elephants cross a swamp their feet sink in so far that if we stepped in one of their footprints we would sink in up to our necks.

Simon has changed companies. I don't want to do the same though I might if Rosslyn stays. One of us will have to go, we are opposites, and have already had differences of opinion. He will organise down to the last detail, and you know how I like being organised.

Simon, like me, did not get on with his company commander who was a particularly stupid man. Rosslyn's planning, though seemingly meticulous, often resulted in chaos. Typical of this was the night the whole company drove to a distant rubber estate to begin an operation at dawn. Rosslyn led the convoy in his jeep and took the left fork when the road divided. The following lorry, and the rest of the convoy, took the right fork so at dawn when we arrived at the estate we were missing our company commander. A meeting of the platoon commanders decided that starting the operation was more important than waiting for Rosslyn, so we dispersed into the jungle. Curiously enough for the remainder of the operation none of our wireless sets was able to receive the urgent messages from base which was trying to arrange a rendezvous with a furious Rosslyn. I think this incident finally convinced the Colonel, who probably guessed that the so-called communications failure was contrived, that it was time that Rosslyn moved to pastures new.

3 NOVEMBER 1953, KOTA BHARU, PANTAI CHINTA BERAHI (BEACH OF PASSIONATE LOVE), KELANTAN, ON A MONTH'S LEAVE

Because of the strain of jungle operations we received five or six days' leave every six weeks, and one month's leave a year.

> I left Lipis at 6.15 a.m. yesterday, and arrived at Krai at 7.15 p.m. What a journey! Thirteen hours in the train, and only 150 miles.

The actual distance was 110 miles, and the average speed was 8½ miles per hour. The steam engines were wood burning and had Indian drivers.

> No food, and the only European on board. What a collection of riff-raff - Malay, Chinese, Tamil, Sikh, Eurasian, smelly, filthy and noisy. Two women decided to breast feed their infants opposite me. A more disgusting sight you couldn't wish for. You know those photos of African women with breasts down to their waists - this was IT! This was the line that General Templer opened - I bet his carriage was a bit different. The train doesn't condescend to make Kota Bharu in one day so I'd planned to taxi the last 40 miles. However, another European got on just before Krai, and I suggested we share a taxi. He said he had a car waiting, and offered me a lift. When we got out of the train a guard of honour presented arms and a lush limousine slid up, all covered with bunting. He was the British Adviser to the Sultan of Kelantan, so I arrived at Kota Bharu in state!

He had been camping in a forest reserve to view the wildlife and looked like a scruffy tramp when he boarded the train. I thought from his appearance that he would welcome my offer to save him money by sharing a taxi, but appearances can be deceptive!

I stayed last night at the officers' mess, 3 Malay, and fixed up my bungalow this morning. It's right on the beach overlooking the South China Sea. The beach is about a mile long with a background of palm trees. Junks and fishing boats come in and out, and the colouring makes the scenery very pretty.

As Rosslyn was out on operations, and Tony away, Ib and I have had long chats. What a life he's had! Captain in the Indian Army at 21, attempted to land in Malaya by submarine (twice) and flying boat. Landed, captured, beaten, pretended to collaborate, misled the Japanese, recommended for a DSO, awarded an MBE and Johore State Medal, marched in Victory Parade in London as a major, introduced the Malay contingent to the Queen (including Chinese resistance leaders now termed 'bandits' and in the jungle with $5,000 rewards on their heads!).

7 NOVEMBER 1953, PANTAI CHINTA BERAHI, ON LEAVE

The Malay Regiment has its married family quarters here at Kota Bharu, and I paid a duty visit to the 6 Malay wives the other day. Lushed up with coffee and biscuits and sherry and beer in return for latest news (discreetly censored by yours truly!) of their husbands. Oh to be a blackmailer! The wives abound with rumours of future battalion moves which certainly I had never heard and which I doubt the colonel has. They have it that we are to retrain in Kota Bharu next year 'so that the husbands can be with their wives'. All very pleasant, but I doubt it.

I was right to doubt it because when the time came we retrained at a camp 200 miles from Kota Bharu!

Several of the wives are English girls married to Malay officers – plus children of varying hues. I would not like to say how the marriages will pan out eventually.

12–30 NOVEMBER 1953, PENANG-TAIPING-KUALA LUMPUR, ON LEAVE

I stayed the first two days at the Paramount Hotel in Penang, but found it too expensive - $12 (£1.40) a day without food. Today I moved to the Mariners' Club, which takes a few single army officers.

The Club soon ran out of space for army officers and I had to depart before my leave was up. The manager recommended a cheap Chinese hotel near the docks in Penang, which turned out to be off-limits for British troops (let alone for officers!). I only realised that it was also a brothel when I kept getting woken up by young Chinese girls knocking on my door at night!

I have now reached the point where the jungle is beginning to sicken me, and I shan't be a bit sorry to say goodbye to it. At first interest overcame discomfort, but this has now changed, how I like comfort! Plenty of experience means I now make myself as comfortable as possible, but there are limits to the discomfort you can avoid. A swamp full of leeches is the same on your hundredth operation as on your first.

I now think that my long leave on glorious beaches had contrasted so sharply with life in the jungle that it had made me temporarily depressed at the prospect of returning to operations.

I was told the other day by a police captain that in the height of the Emergency it was noticeable that planters who treated their workers well were the first to be murdered, the others unknowingly helping the communist cause by causing discontent. A sad commentary on communism's moral standards.

Chin Peng, of course, had a different version of events, claiming that the planters killed by his men had treated their workers badly.[17] During the early years of the Emergency about one in ten planters were murdered.[18]

The Japanese who went into the jungle (or never came out) with the Reds are gradually being whittled down. About fifty at the start, they are now down to a dozen (these include a doctor living in the jungle near Lipis) and are used as instructors. The first question asked a surrendered bandit by Special Branch is: 'Do you know of any white bandits?' The police say the answer is always 'No', but there is, however, room for doubt.

The Emergency in its present state is likely to continue for a long time yet, gradually improving. I saw the figures to date - about 5,000 bandits killed, 1,000 surrendered. About 6,000 went into the jungle in 1948, and there are about the same number in today. Complete turnover, by numbers anyway.

The first two figures I quoted were reasonably accurate as the official estimates of terrorist eliminations between 1948 and 1953 are 4,833 killed and 1,284 surrendered. Omitted from the figures are 1,064 who were captured, and an unknown number who died of wounds, starvation or sickness, or were executed by their own side, or who deserted. Other estimates of the numbers in the jungle in 1948 and 1953 are lower than my figure of 6,000, being 4,000–5,000 in 1948 and 5,500 in 1953. Estimates of the greatest number of terrorists ever range from 8,000 to 10,000 in 1951.[19]

I think Rosslyn will be leaving B Company soon. The colonel has at last caught up with him and wants him to move; this will stop me asking for a posting for the time.

The dropping of rum to the Malay Regiment is a mystery to me, still, not a word to the authorities!

Did those responsible for specifying the contents of the cargoes to be dropped not know that Malays, being Muslims, were not allowed to drink alcohol? If they did know, perhaps the presence of British officers in the regiment was held to justify the alcohol.

1 DECEMBER 1953, LIPIS

I admire Rosslyn as an organiser; he's a wonderful officer provided he doesn't come in contact with human beings. Written orders and 'systems' are his forte, not man management.

I think I used the words 'admire' and 'wonderful' only to spice up the crushing proviso which followed.

It's difficult to say about the bravery of Malay troops. Having never served with English troops in action I can't compare. Probably like all armies some are good and others aren't. I'd trust my life to a half dozen of my platoon, and not to another half dozen. The rest?

I sometimes wondered what would happen if I was leading a patrol when we were surrounded by a large number of terrorists who offered to let my men escape with their lives if they handed me over. At least one captured British soldier was reported to have been skinned alive so the prospect of being captured was very worrying.[20] Surrender demands were made in 1950 when a large group of terrorists ambushed a platoon of 3 Malay, which was commanded by a Malay subaltern who was killed in the opening burst of fire, leaving a corporal to take command. The terrorists called on the soldiers to surrender four times, but each time the soldiers responded with fire. Fifteen soldiers were killed, three others later died of wounds, six more were wounded and three unwounded men were captured. The terrorist leader lectured the survivors on their foolishness in fighting the MRLA, instructed them to leave the Army, and then released them. It was thought from the graves found by the Army follow-up party that at least twenty-nine terrorists had been killed during the incident.[21]

Later this month I had a nasty shock. I had gone to the local police station to listen to a captured terrorist being interrogated. When I entered the room he looked round at me, and then flung himself at my feet. Clutching me round the knees, he began wailing in Cantonese which I did not understand. While he was being dragged back to his chair I asked the interpreter what it was all about. 'He was begging you to save his life,' he said. 'What makes him think I'd want to do that?' I asked. 'Because he says he once saved yours.' Startled, I asked for details. After questioning him the interpreter said: 'He and three comrades were on the south bank of the Sungai Jelai River last month when you and your platoon arrived on the other bank. While your men brewed tea you sat on the bank studying a map, having taken off your boots to dangle your feet in the river. His comrades wanted to shoot you, but he stopped them'. I remembered the occasion because it was the only time I had ever bothered to take off my boots to cool my feet in a river during our hourly ten minute rests. Astounded at my close shave, I asked why the prisoner had stopped his men from firing; 'Because he knew that if they killed a British officer there would be a massive Army follow-up which would make their lives a misery for weeks.' The prisoner was later charged with setting fire to a bus load of Malay school children from a village which had refused to give food to his gang. He was tried, found guilty, and hanged. If he had given in to his comrades' desire to shoot me, and if their rifles and ammunition had been in good condition, and their marksmanship adequate for 50ft (not all of these requirements were possessed by every terrorist), then I would have missed the fifty years I have subsequently enjoyed. Ever since this incident I have believed that the importance of luck as a factor in life is frequently underestimated.

1 The author in 1954 and 2004.

2 The author in 2004.

3 C Company, Eaton Hall Officer Cadet School, 1953. The author in the second row from the back, first on the left.

4 The slogan at Tras.

5 Lieutenant 'Busty' Hussein.

6 The author, 1953.

7 *Left:* The Chinese headman of Jerkoh New Village.

8 *Below left:* A terrorist authentication stamp.

9 *Below right:* An imprint of the terrorist authentication stamp.

10a and 10b *Above and below:* River crossing.

11 S-55 Naval helicopter getting in.

12 S-55 Naval helicopter getting there.

13 S-55 Naval helicopter getting down.

14 S55 Naval helicopter getting out.

15 Platoon's NCOs.

16 *Opposite above:* Operation Fraser's Hill, Sergeant Manaf.

17 *Opposite midle:* Operation Fraser's Hill, the author.

18 *Opposite below:* Operation Fraser's Hill, the author on the same rock, 1985.

19 Operation Fraser's Hill, Ujang batman.

20 Operation Fraser's Hill, Private Ibrahim.

21 Operation Fraser's Hill, the author.

22 *Above:* A 6 Malay Christmas card, 1953.

23a and 23b *Above and below:* A $100 note of Japanese 'banana' money.

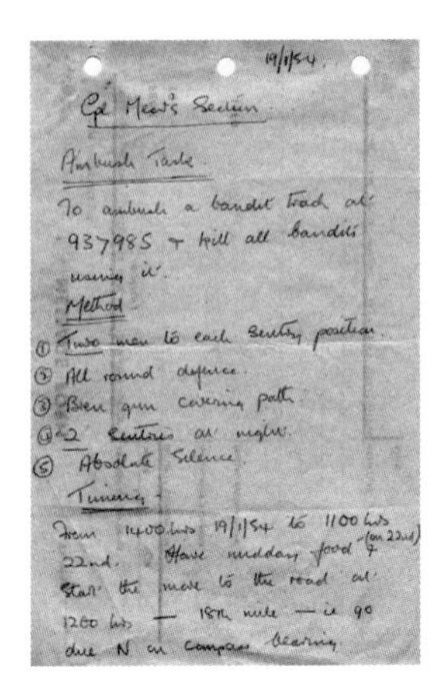

19/1/54.

Cpl Meor's Section

Ambush Task

To ambush a bandit track at 937985 + kill all bandits using it.

Method

1. Two men to each sentry position.
2. All round defence.
3. Bren gun covering path.
4. 2 sentries at night.
5. Absolute silence.

Timing –

From 1400 hrs 19/1/54 to 1100 hrs 22nd. Have midday food (on 22nd) + start the move to the road at 1200 hrs — 18th mile — ie go due N on compass bearing

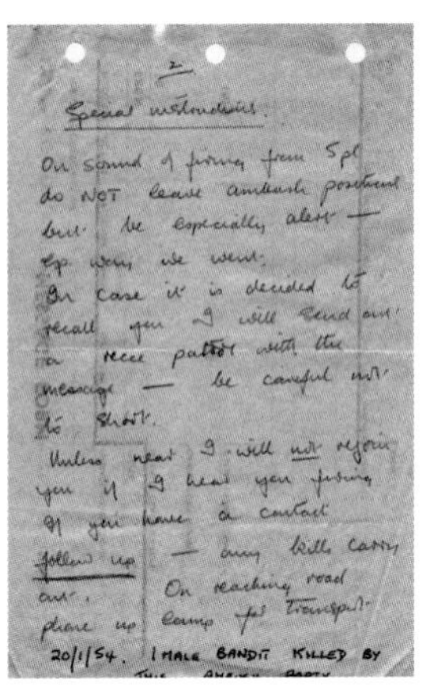

2

Special instructions.

On sound of firing from 5 pl do NOT leave ambush position but be especially alert — [illegible] we went.

In case it is decided to recall you I will send out a recce patrol with the message — be careful not to shoot.

Unless near I will not rejoin you if I hear you firing.

If you have a contact follow up — any kills carry out. On reaching road phone up camp for transport.

20/1/54. 1 MALE BANDIT KILLED BY THE AMBUSH PARTY

24 Corporal Meor's ambush orders.

25 Operation Fraser's Hill, the author, 1953.

26 Operation Fraser's Hill, jungle views, 1985.

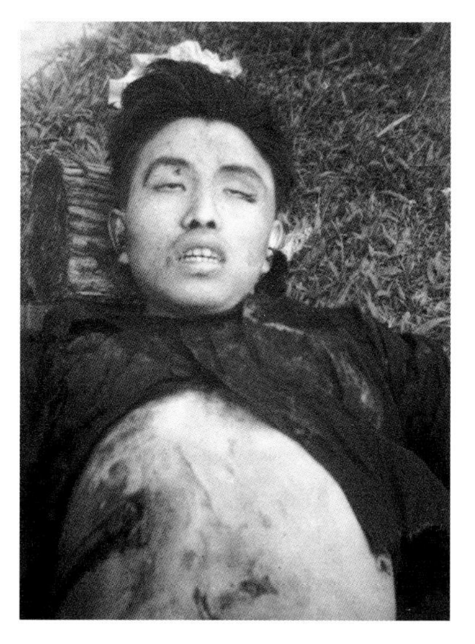

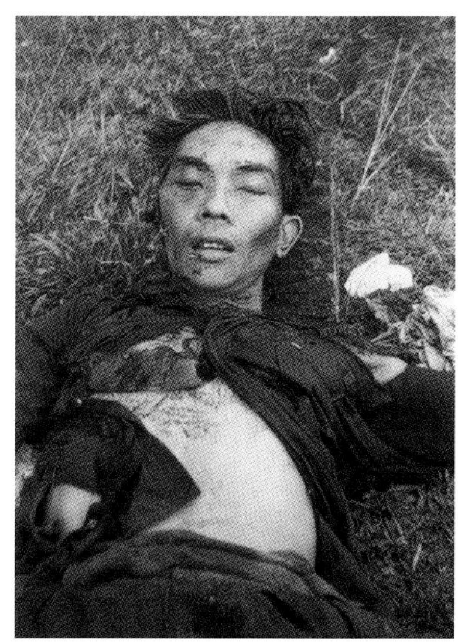

27 *Above left:* Lim Men Sek.

28 *Above right:* Chan Ban Sin.

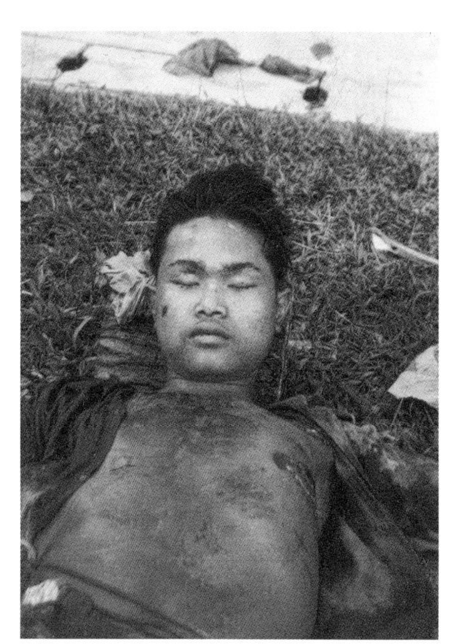

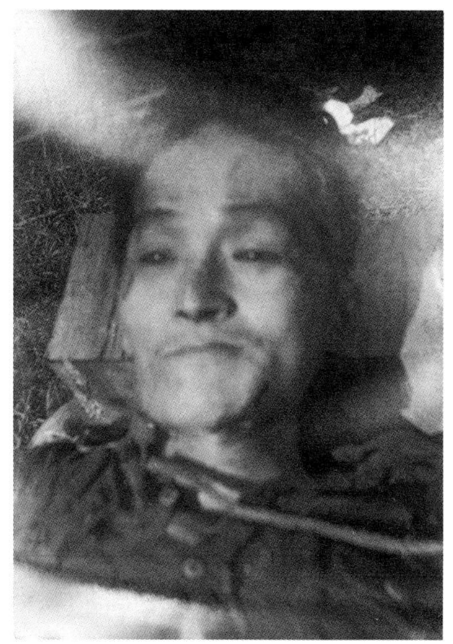

29 *Above left:* Ah Wei.

30 *Above right:* Sani bin Mat Buscut.

31 B Company's officers. From left to right: Tony, Rosslyn, the author, Fletcher.

32 5 Platoon, B Company. The author is seated behind the shield.

33 Ib and the author, London, 1955.

34 Sergeant Abdul Manaf MM, 1956.

35 *Left:* Major Roy Fletcher, 1957.

36 *Below:* Simon Pritchard and the author, Port Dickson, 2003.

I later discovered that my experience was certainly not unique. Tony Froom had been told by a surrendered terrorist that he and two comrades had seen him and his batman examining one of their cultivations in the jungle, but had not shot him because they thought the rest of his men must be close nearby (actually they were making camp some distance away). In 1950 a terrorist disclosed that on four previous occasions he had seen the subaltern who had led the platoon which had eventually captured him.[22] How many other British officers had been held in the sights of terrorist rifles, but had escaped death because of fears of retribution? And how many ever learned of their good luck? Ignorance can certainly be bliss!

4 DECEMBER 1953, ULU JELAI

Just returned from an abortive night ambush. We had a guide who didn't admit he was uncertain of his way until 1.00 a.m. when he'd satisfactorily lost us. What a war! I took in ten men and left camp at 8.30 p.m. It was a pitch black night, and for two hours we ploughed through overgrown rubber plantations holding our hands up so the man behind could see the luminosity on our wristwatches. Luminous leaves and fireflies confused the issue, and I and eight men followed a big firefly for some time before I realised it was not the man in front of me! I won't mention the resulting confusion and bad language! Patches of luminous leaves throw sufficient light to show up details and look like patches of cold green sunlight.

I slept like a babe till 5.30 a.m. in the open, a shade cool towards dawn. On returning this morning I was horrified to see the narrow planks over rivers I'd felt my way along the night before. Still, what the eye doesn't see…

9 DECEMBER 1953, NEAR FRASER'S HILL

The map on page 99 shows the route we took during this operation.

In spite of the address, not on leave I'm afraid. Far from it, on an operation in the mountains. We are after some bandits who ambushed the road near where they killed Gurney. Cheeky blighters even laid a mine! It didn't go off, and they ran. Muggins is after them (three days and probably 20 miles behind).

Sir Henry Gurney, the High Commissioner, was killed in 1951 in an ambush set up by Siew Ma who commanded an independent platoon of thirty-six terrorists. Gurney was in his Rolls-Royce with his wife, secretary and chauffeur on their way to spend a weekend at the holiday resort of Fraser's Hill. Their police escort was pathetically inadequate. An unarmoured open Land Rover with five Malay policemen not armed with automatic weapons led, followed by the Rolls, followed by a radio van with a scout car bringing up the rear. Half way into their journey the radio van broke down and the scout car lost contact with the Rolls.

On the winding road close to Fraser's Hill the terrorists waited on top of a 20ft-high bank, and when they opened fire with two Bren guns all except one of the policemen in the Land Rover were wounded, as was the chauffeur of the Rolls which stopped. Gurney opened the door on the side facing the terrorists, stepped out, closed the door, and walked towards the bank. Before he reached it he was shot dead. He had been an infantry officer in the First World War and had been wounded, and the author of the article about him in the new edition of the *Dictionary of National Biography* described him as 'courageous and composed to the last' and states that he 'got out of the car to draw the fire away from his wife and secretary'. When the scout car belatedly arrived and opened fire the terrorists vanished into the jungle having suffered no casualties. A massive Army follow-up involving three battalions failed to catch them. Siew Ma had intended to attack a military convoy to seize weapons, so Gurney's death was unplanned though the propaganda triumph for the terrorists was immense. Gurney had persistently refused to have large escorts and to travel in armoured vehicles, but he should have had an armoured car leading the Rolls. Siew Ma survived until 1959 when he was betrayed by his bodyguards and shot by a patrol.[23] The Gurney ambush had two ironic features. First, Siew Ma had been taught ambushing by the British Army in 1942.[24] Secondly, in 1950 Gurney had announced that the Emergency must be brought to an end in 1951.[25] Sadly, it was he who was brought to an end in 1951 while the Emergency continued for another nine years.

> We camped the first night at 1,600 feet with a glorious view over Pahang. The following day we climbed to 3,800 feet in only 3,000 yards, a gradient of one in four. It took us all day, mostly on hands and knees. Waterfalls galore and sheer rock faces, like the Lost World. Shan't be surprised to see a dinosaur any time here. It's noticeably cooler up here, but it has no effect on the vegetation, thicker if anything.

One day we reached a shallow river gushing swiftly down a smooth but steep bed of rock. There were boulders on either side, so the easiest route seemed to be up the bed of the river. I got some way up before slipping

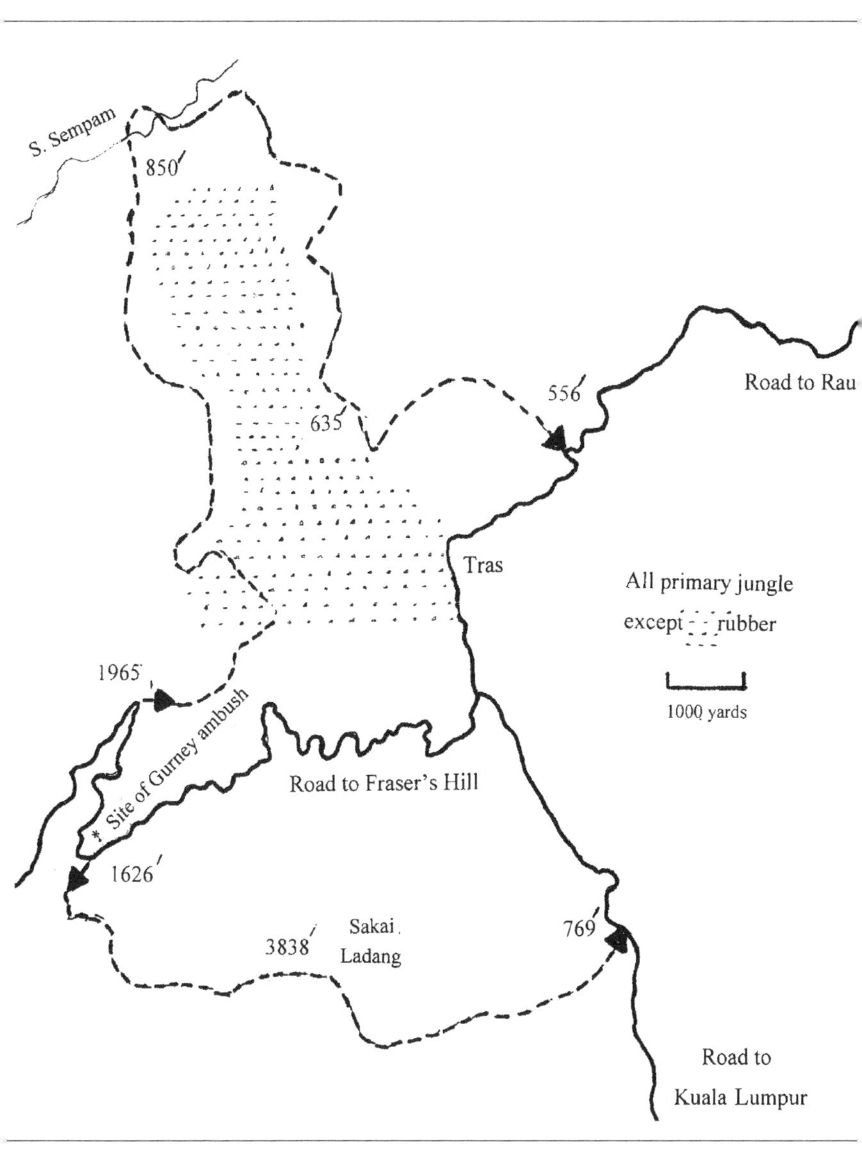

Operation Fraser's Hill.

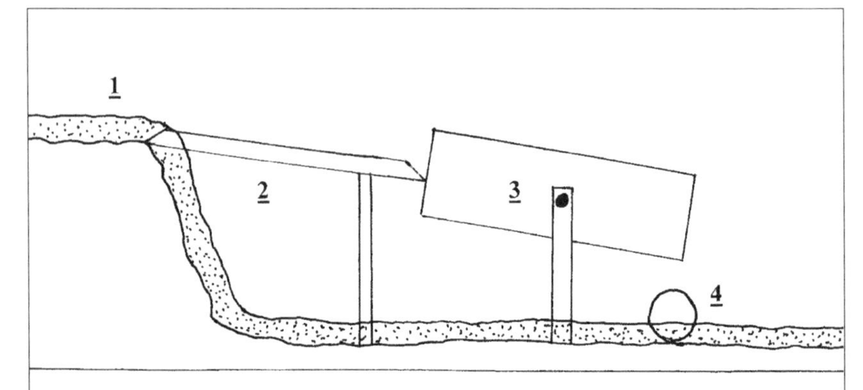

1 THE STREAM WATER RUNS INTO 2 A BAMBOO PIPE WHICH DIRECTS IT INTO 3 A BIG BAMBOO STEM BLOCKED UP HALF WAY ALONG AND SWINGING ON AN AXLE. WHEN THE WATER FILLS THE LEFT HAND HALF OF THE STEM IT DROPS AND THE WATER RUNS OUT. THIS HALF THEN RISES CAUSING THE RIGHT HAND HALF (WHICH IS WEIGHTED INSIDE) TO DROP AND HIT 4 ANOTHER BAMBOO STEM AND THIS MAKES THE SOUND 'BONG'. THIS PROCESS IS THEN REPEATED.

Sakai sounding device.

on some slime, falling backwards, hitting my head and sliding back down to my point of entry where my sergeant hauled me out. I still have a lump on the back of my head as a souvenir.

Camping last night at 3,838 feet we had no water so the boys tapped the bamboo stems. Each stem holds over a pint of water so we had a drink after all. On the few occasions we get a view it's panoramic, weather good so far, and really lovely country - as long as you don't have to march in it!

Today we started going downhill, as difficult as going up. Felt like Tarzan on occasion while swinging from creeper to creeper. Sheer rock faces and dense vegetation, rivers plunging 20 feet in waterfalls, all very primary. No humans live here (except bandits) not even Aborigines. Plenty of wild pig, tiger and porcupines, towering trees, and hundreds of mosquitoes. Pretty cold at night. I sleep in two pairs of everything and a sarong, and am still cold. Not surprising considering we are as high as Snowdon.

10th I was wrong about there being no Aborigines. We came across a Sakai ladang (Aboriginal cultivation) bananas, tapioca, etc. It has a very clever signalling device to guide hunters back to the clearing. It consists of bamboo which goes bong, bong, every 20 seconds - a noise which can be heard for some long way. Very ingenious!

How could such primitive people have invented perpetual motion? Elsewhere in Pahang, Aborigines built musical windmills with large wooden sails and bamboo flutes, which made noises like 'Ho-hu, ho-hu' when the wind blew. They placed them in tall trees, and they may have been intended to scare away devils.[26] The device we found probably had a similar purpose as Aboriginal hunters did not need it to find their way back to their ladang as they knew the surrounding country like the back of their hands.

11th Having come right over the mountains HQ has finally decided the bandits went the other way, so, restocked with food, we are ploughing through another lot of mountains. Just camped for the evening by a big waterfall. Have been swimming in the pool below, the rush of water is very invigorating. The stones are rounded, and one can let oneself be carried down 20 yards and then swim up again. This morning I caught a huge (six inch wingspan) blue and black butterfly, the biggest I've ever seen. Hope to bring it out safely with me, it's a whopper! The best way to catch them out here is to get the men to put out their socks to dry on the rocks. A nice smelly old sock is a sure attraction. I've seen one particularly high sock absolutely covered with big green and blue butterflies.

The attraction was the salt in the sweat.

At 8.00 a.m. we got a fine view over the mountains, each one cloud-capped (we were higher than the distant mountains when we started). It's the sort of scene that if you painted it no one would believe you (like Turner's sunsets). Alternate white clouds and green jungle in layers stretching into the distance.

12th We have a surrendered bandit with us this operation - a little man who answers to George or Claud (real name Li something). About a year ago he was in a camp which my sergeant attacked with eight men. The 20-odd bandits (including George) all ran. While discussing this coincidence George said: 'I left my watch behind'. Manaf: 'I found a watch there, is this it?' George: 'Yes!' He then suggested that Manaf handed it over. Manaf: 'How much did you get for surrendering?' George: '$500'. Manaf: 'Then you could afford to buy it back.' Negotiations are proceeding. Our chaps are always a little bitter about the bandits getting $500 for surrendering.

16th Was very glad to get mail airdropped in with our food. Am now searching yet another lot of ruddy jungle. Operation finishes on 18th, my wireless has broken down, so I've got to finish then, thank goodness (can't get more food).

Rosslyn is definitely leaving B Company next month. Hope his successor is better.

Had a Xmas card airdropped in. Strange to see pictures of snow in the jungle, the boys were mystified!

A British subaltern friend in 6 Malay is in hospital, wounded in the bottom by a piece of 25 pounder shrapnel. The Royal Artillery were firing into a bandit camp, and he was to do the attack. He started off a shade prematurely, and stopped a bulls eye in his bottom. Oh the language! He left by helicopter (clutching his posterior) for Xmas with the nurses (standing up!). He was actually shouting: 'Come on men, follow me, there's nothing to be afraid of!', when events sharply proved him wrong.

The amusing aftermath of this incident is described in the Epilogue.

Officers who shout encouragement to their men sometimes immediately suffer setbacks, though it is fortunate that not all of these are serious. One example concerned an officer who was taking part in the invasion of North Africa in 1942. As his landing craft approached the beach he shouted to his men 'Follow me!' before prematurely leaping from the lowered ramp and disappearing beneath the waves. Dripping with seaweed, he struggled ashore, where his men, dry shod, awaited him.[27]

That Kenyan officer got off on a technicality - he was as guilty as hell. His CO has also finished his career through this.

This presumably referred to a British army officer who had been court martialled for deliberately killing innocent Kenyans during operations against the Mau Mau terrorists in order to raise his unit's score. The insurrection in Kenya had begun in the early 1950s when the Kikuyu tribe claimed that the white men had stolen their land (though in fact they had long since sold nearly all of it to another African tribe). An Emergency was declared in 1952, but lasted only until 1956.[28] During the fighting the Mau Mau killed about 2,500 people, nearly all of whom were African, and their losses totalled some 10,000 killed and 2,600 captured.[29] Although the leaders of the Kikuyu now praise the Mau Mau insurrection for hastening the grant of independence, the level of corruption and dictatorship in present-day Kenya suggests that a continuation of British colonialism would have been better for the people.

It's a great temptation for units to build up a big score via a few 'mistakes'. It has happened out here, but 99 per cent of officers are quite rightly dead against it. Mistakes do happen (a subaltern friend shot and killed a tapper) but bloody-mindedness like this is awful.

An atrocity was committed by British soldiers in December 1948, when a fouteen-man patrol of Scots Guards led by a sergeant shot and killed twenty-four Chinese villagers who were allegedly terrorists trying to escape after being captured. The evidence that this was a massacre of innocents includes the fact that all were killed and none were wounded, the lack of any captured weapons, the official wall of silence which descended instead of the wide publicity which would have followed such a military triumph, the admission in 1970 by four members of the patrol that the Chinese had been massacred and had not been trying to escape, a similar confession made to Scotland Yard in 1992 by a member of the patrol, and a statement made in 1993 by the sole survivor of the massacre.

The public in Malaya had expressed their suspicions at the time, and the country's Attorney-General ordered an enquiry which concluded that 'a bona fide mistake had been made', but none of the evidence taken at the enquiry was ever made public. The sergeant probably carried out the massacre to win promotion or a decoration, and those who failed to bring him to justice were as guilty as he was. This massacre was on a tiny scale compared with that carried out at My Lai in Vietnam by US soldiers in 1968, when hundreds of civilians were reportedly killed, but it was news of the My Lai massacre which led to a tip-off to the *People* newspaper that a similar incident had occurred in Malaya, and this led to an investigation which exposed the truth, but did not result in justice being done.[30]

Big stir last night - my batman was bitten by a ruddy great black scorpion. It crawled into bed with him and stung him through his trousers. I chopped it in half, gave him three

green pills (what they are really for no one knows!) dabbed him with iodine and gave him a stiff shot of rum. He was very frightened, and asked: 'Will I lose my leg, Tuan?' to which I replied that I'd been bitten by scorpions twice as big as this in England without ill effects (the lie of the year!). He was OK next day, thanks be.

Over the years I am sure many sick soldiers have been given the wrong pills. In 1914, Field Ambulance units were issued with pills which had numbers on them which indicated that they were for specific ailments, and number nine was for constipation. One constipated soldier went to a unit which had run out of number nines and was given a number five and a number four instead.[31]

The scorpion was a most repulsive looking thing about a foot long. The platoon spent two hours searching for 'his friend', believing two always go together, without result.

19th Arrived back last night after 12 days out. Rosslyn met three bandits, but I had no contact. Rained like hell the last few days. New major already arrived, seems OK.

Notes

1 Chin Peng, p.91.
2 Crockett, p.65.
3 Holman, p.19; Spencer Chapman, *The Jungle*, p.131.
4 Barber, p.154.
5 Cloake, pp.24, 94, 139.
6 Miller, *Jungle*, pp.145-47.
7 Short, p.210.
8 Ibid., pp.214-16.
9 Spencer Chapman, *The Jungle*, pp.58-59.
10 Barber, p.196.
11 Short, p.507.
12 16 January 1992, p.19.
13 Chin Peng, p.135.
14 Kennedy, p.260.
15 Campbell, p.5.
16 Chin Peng, p.307.
17 Ibid., p.511.
18 Gullick, p.98.
19 R. Thompson, p.47; Short, pp.349, 472, 507.
20 Miller, *Jungle*, p.56. I have found no confirmation of this claim of skinning alive.

21 Ibid., pp.65-68.
22 Scurr, p.255.
23 Short pp.303-05; Barber, pp.131-2; A. Chin, p.37; Miller, *Jungle* p.196; DNB, Vol. 24, p.281; Chin Peng, pp.287, 294.
24 Chin Peng, p.287.
25 Short, p.252.
26 Miller, *Menace*, p.127; Spencer Chapman, *The Jungle*, p.188.
27 *The Daily Telegraph*, 10 November 2004, p.27, the obituary of Jack Wolff.
28 Ibid., 27 August 2004, p.29, the obituary of Paul Ngei, an ex-Mau Mau leader.
29 Neillands, *A Fighting Retreat*, p.203
30 Barber, pp.79-80; Short, pp.166-69; *The Daily Telegraph*, 19 August 1993, p.21; Chin Peng, pp.239-40.
31 van Emden, p.20.

CHAPTER 5

Jungle Operations and Leave: 26 December 1953–23 July 1954

26 DECEMBER 1953, LIPIS

Illustration number 22 in the picture section shows the battalion's Christmas card.

> I've been up with the RAF several times in their Auster spotter aircraft, a single engine monoplane two-seater that cruises at about 80 mph. The jungle from about 1,000 feet looks like a series of blue-grey cotton wool balls packed tightly together, rivers almost invisible, and hills tiny.

The seating arrangements for passengers in Austers were primitive. On one of my trips the turbulence caused the plane to buck so I held on to a wire that ran above my head, in order to help me stay in my seat behind the pilot. He began wrestling with the controls, but the plane began to tip sideways so I gripped the wire tighter. Only when he turned his head to warn me about the possible need for an emergency landing did he see that I was gripping the wire which apparently controlled the tail. Calm returned when I let go.

> Yesterday, Xmas Day, the British officers in Lipis played the British sergeants at football in fancy dress. Rosslyn and I went as bandits wearing genuine red-starred peak hats, khaki, and long puttees. We were carried on stretchers by eight stalwarts, and played with hockey sticks. The brigadier turned up in football boots, pyjamas and a policeman's helmet, all of which he quickly lost. The troops seemed to have enjoyed it thoroughly. It rained heavily beforehand and the field was a mass of mud. The brigade major's face was rammed in the mud by the regimental sergeant-major who was later thrown in the water tank.

The brigade major was generally disliked, and three months later, when we heard that HMT *Empire Windrush*, on which he was returning to England, had sunk in the Mediterranean after a boiler explosion, the whole mess cheered. He survived, as did nearly everyone else on board, but his kit did not.

> **After this, we entertained the sergeants to drinks at the brigade officer's mess, and then went down to the British troops' cookhouse and served them their Xmas lunch. We had a Xmas party in the mess in the evening.**

At this party an Englishman in civilian clothes came up to me and said: 'London School of Economics, 1952.' Astonished, I asked how he knew. 'MI5,' he replied. 'I saw you in the college library when I was checking the politics of those students who were likely to become National Service officers'. I had then been very interested in politics, and though I held right-wing views I had considered joining every political society at LSE in order to listen to all their debates. Had I done so, and if this man was telling the truth, my membership of the communist society would have ruled out all hope of a commission. An example of how some in the Army regarded LSE at the time was provided by a Royal Army Education Corps officer in 1959, when he told his students that he didn't want 'any dirty-pink LSE types' in his corps.

I remain unsure about the truth of the party guest's story, although there are two pieces of circumstantial evidence which support it. First, LSE had a very left-wing reputation in the early 1950s and a strong communist party membership amongst the students. Secondly, ex-members of MI5 were certainly working in Special Branch in Malaya at the time of our conversation.[2] Anyway, if the story was not true, why would he have bothered to invent it?

Because of the many guests at the party, and the expected high level of liquid consumption, a temporary additional urinal consisting of an oil drum partly filled with water had been placed outside behind the mess, with some empty beer crates alongside to provide steps so that the guests could place the necessary part over the edge of the drum. Before the party got underway, some joker released into the water some baby crocodiles which could always be bought from a shop in Lipis. Later on in the evening, the level of liquid had risen so high that one guest was only just able to snatch his vital part away from a set of snapping jaws in time. Nobody believed him when he rushed back to the mess to sound the alarm, but a recce party confirmed his story.

Two nights ago we had a riot in the town - B Company stormed the police station. Our riot all started with an argument between a soldier and a policeman over the soldier's wife. Several policemen beat up my chap, who ran to the cinema and called out about 100 of my chaps who, driving the police through the market, proceeded to lay siege to the police station. This was not done in a spirit of fun, but in deadly earnest, revolvers were fired and knives used. Rosslyn was away, and I was called down by a hysterical police officer who said he was under bombardment in the police station by my chaps. I roared down in an armoured car with four troops with fixed bayonets just in time to stop the police setting up a machine gun. Glad to report my presence calmed my chaps, and after laying about with my heavy electric torch (one knocked out - a policeman - and two stunned) I fell them in and doubled them back to camp. I arrived back in camp just in time to intercept a squad of my platoon heading for the police station with a 2 inch mortar and ten high explosive bombs!

All this may sound incredible, but the Malay temperament when roused produces this sort of result.

Normally, the Malays are peaceful and easy going, but when angered they can run amok, this being an English word appropriately derived from the Malay word 'amoq' – rushing in frenzy.

Last year in 3 Malay the officer arrived too late, and the troops had already fired three grenades into the police station, two killed and one injured. Shouts of 'Blood will run tonight!' hotted up the evening's entertainment. The total Chinese population of Lipis retreated upstairs to watch their arch-enemies the Malays fighting it out, with obvious delight.

While I was laying about with my torch, a man on the first-floor balcony of one of the Chinese houses shouted: 'Kill that Englishman'. This instruction was, fortunately, ignored, and the shout merely confirmed what I already knew, namely that most of the town's Malayan Chinese inhabitants supported the communists. Before the British returned to Malaya, following the Japanese surrender in 1945, the MPAJA had taken control of the town.[3]

The fool of a British police officer couldn't get a grip on his men, who unlocked the arms store and issued rifles all

round - 10 minutes later and phew! My chaps have twice the discipline of the police, and went quietly. We have the leading lights under arrest (that police officer should be too - my batman caught him a terrific crack over the head with a club so I suppose it's all square!). They calm down very quickly, and we allowed them in town last night with no trouble, an amazing people. The veneer of civilised behaviour is very thin and an occasional storming of a police station or village is not regarded in the serious light we do at home. All the Army has done is teach them that a Bren gun is a rather more effective weapon than a parang. Any trouble and they all head back to camp for mortars, machine guns, etc. A rather neat right flanking movement was carried out by my platoon which, under different circumstances, would have been a joy to see. Happy days! No one seriously hurt, and promises never to let it happen again - some hopes!

Apart from this incident I found that commanding my platoon was trouble free as none of the 40 men committed any of the military offences sometimes encountered in the British Army, namely absence without leave, idleness on parade and being drunk and disorderly. I think that this excellent record resulted from the good characters of the men and the discipline maintained by my strong minded sergeant. Still, had I failed to intercept the squad bringing the mortar to bomb the police station the resulting offence would have been rather more serious than those sometimes encountered in the British Army.

30 DECEMBER 1953, SUNGAI KERUPAN/SUNGAI KETIR

Got back from a two day operation last night. We went in and out by train which saved a lot of walking. The 'bandit camp' turned out to be an old Sakai village of eight houses, and the 'bandit tracks' were elephant made.

Another typical example of the quality of the information fed to the Army by the police. Tracks made by elephants are always marked by numerous broken branches, felled trees and mountains of dung. Terrorists always tried hard to eradicate all signs that they had made a track. Did the police informant not know these well-known facts? Why did the police not ask him to describe the 'bandit' tracks?

We suffered from the attentions of thousands of biting sandflies, and I'm itching all over. Heavy rain also did not improve the comfort. We've had heavy rain ever since Xmas and parts of Lipis are flooded. Rosslyn is ill so my leave is delayed for a week or so. Major Fletcher (new company commander) takes over on or about 10 January. I am being very careful about ambushes - a friend of mine was killed last week in an ambush.

31st Just heard that retraining and the new base will begin early in April at Mentakab in Pahang - an absolute blank blank of a dead end, one eyed, back of beyond, coal heap.

I was orderly officer that evening when the phone rang in the Brigade mess and a grating voice demanded: 'How much rum have you got?' I thought it was one of our local drunken planters on the scrounge for some free booze. 'Plenty, thank you,' I replied, hung up, and returned to my game of liar dice. Ten minutes later the phone rang again, and a smooth voice said 'I'm ADC to the Quartermaster General. I'd like to speak to the young officer who has just been talking to the general about the brigade's stock of rum for airdropping to the troops.' I explained that unfortunately the officer concerned had just left the mess to go on a long operation. 'Get him to ring me when he gets back,' I was told, but strangely enough he never did.

12 JANUARY 1954, KUALA LUMPUR, ON SIX DAY'S LEAVE STAYING WITH A FRIEND IN THE RASC MESS

Rosslyn has left to command HQ company.

Despite the bravery demonstrated by his award of the MC, Rosslyn should not have stayed in the Army as he had no man-management skills, and was not fit enough to cope with active service. He was frequently ill during 1953, and just before he left us Tony awoke one night on hearing his name being called out. He got up to investigate, and found Rosslyn sitting in the officers' toilet which was some way downhill from our quarters. He was too weak to move, and Tony (a big strong man) carried him back to bed and summoned the Brigade medical officer. Tony later told me that Rosslyn 'was just a bag of bones.'

Roy Fletcher, 14th/20th King's Hussars, tank experience in desert, very senior major, no infantry experience, very fond of the bottle, vast fund of amusing stories, very sensible, and going to be well liked by the men.

This rapid assessment of the new company commander proved to be absolutely accurate. What always surprised me was that when Roy planned an operation, usually in ten minutes and with a large glass of scotch in his hand, it nearly always went well, while Rosslyn's planning took hours and often went wrong.

When Rosslyn handed over we had a parade in regimental parade dress. In the evening we had a bonfire party with ronggeng and joget (dancing).

The band of the Royal West Kents paid a week's visit to Lipis. Beat retreat in the town before an astonished Malay and Chinese crowd, and played at a dinner night and cocktail party in the officer's mess, and at a sergeants' mess dance.

We had three tiring, boozy parties in a row with a rather high-powered set of exalted military personages - a Brigadier, four Colonels and a dozen Majors. I waited till our Colonel was well set on champagne cocktails and then touched him for this leave. I'm sure he didn't know what I was asking for, so I shot away to Kuala Lumpur very smartly yesterday before he recovered! I'm entitled to the leave, but had pre-warning of a long operation that was likely to postpone it.

The papers out here are full of nonsense about 'The Thing'. All it is is an orang-outang, a smallish ape, able to chatter, having a bare face and certain human characteristics. It's quite rare and rather fierce, superstition does the rest.

The local newspapers had reported that three people on the edge of a rubber estate in Perak had seen three large, blond, human creatures with reddish hair shambling away into the trees. Speculation at the time was of 'lost tribes' and 'ape-men'. My assertion of orang-utan is supported by the claim of reddish hair which is a feature of this ape.[4]

I was in the local police station last week when they brought in a boy of 11 caught carrying $500 of opium in tiny packets. Brown treacly-like stuff, said he'd found it in the street!

I was given a packet which I smoked in my pipe. No lovely dreams, but a splitting headache. Terrorists escorted opium-smugglers from Siam into Malaya to raise money.[5]

17 JANUARY 1954, LIPIS

I flew up from Kuala Lumpur to avoid the fatigue of the 120 mile drive over the Gap road. The plane was a small six-seater, and as I was the only passenger I sat next to the pilot.

Sand-flies are much worse than leeches. With leeches you can see them and burn them off, and they don't hurt. Sand-flies are too small to see, bite like hell, and itch like fury. They penetrate ordinary trousers so there's no defence. Give me a leech any day!

21 JANUARY 1954, ULU DONG

The map opposite shows the route we took on this operation.

The third day of a six day operation. A touch of excitement this operation - we met some bandits. I dropped off one section to ambush a track while I carried on with two sections. Following a track we were fired on by a bandit sentry, who then ran for his life. We lost him in the thick jungle, and arrived at his camp just in time to see the last bandit running out.

Although I always tried to keep alert while on operations, the infrequency of contacts and the heat and fatigue meant that after several hours of trekking, the mind began to wander in the direction of future pleasures. Thus the totally unexpected loud bang from a terrorist sentry's shotgun close in front was a heart-stopping moment. The *Army Handbook* was clear on what should then be done – an immediate assault on the terrorist camp. Unfortunately it did not tell us where the camp was. Sixty yards in front? Thirty yards to the left? Up hill? Down hill? In practice the platoon commander really had only one option – yell 'Charge!' and rush straight ahead. This I did, and as I reached the camp I fired at the last terrorist who was running out. I hoped he would drop dead, but he vanished into the bushes. After it was all over I discovered how he had escaped (assuming my aim had been accurate which, given my eyesight, was somewhat unlikely) – the bullet from my carbine had lodged in a thick liana which was hanging down between us.

We gave chase, but lost them. I was furious, but the boys did their best. We'd disturbed the bandits whilst they were cooking their midday meal - dried bananas, bamboo shoots and decayed pig. We recovered six pairs of trousers, six pairs

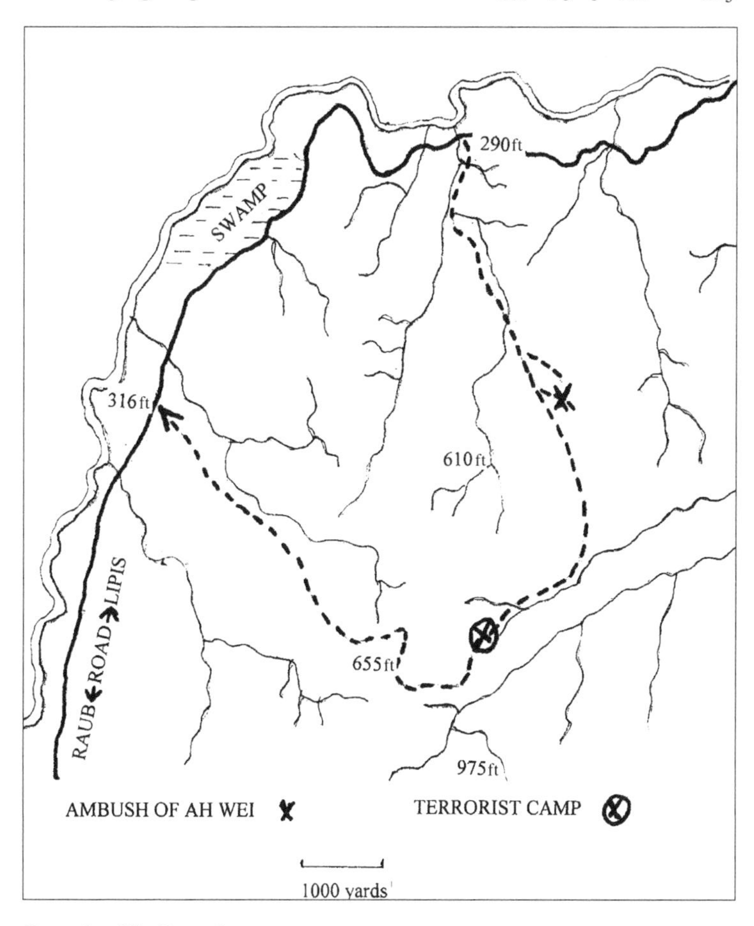

Operation Ulu Dong, January 1954.

of shoes, and three red-starred hats, so once again there's a party of nude bandits in Pahang.

Terrorists fleeing camps often left clothing behind, and in the battalion this was known as 'debagging'. Though the clothes were not easily replaced, and their loss must have lowered morale, our Colonel was not impressed by bundles of trousers and wanted bundles of bodies instead. Chasing terrorists out of camps could be dangerous, and not only because of the risk of being ambushed. While doing so, Tommy once fell up to his neck into a terrorist latrine.

We found a copy of the Koran, and bandit propaganda books in Chinese, so they were a mixed party.

The terrorists faced a major problem in recruiting Malays because they were Muslims and Marxism does not accept religions. To try to overcome this difficulty the leadership of the MCP was 'careful not to even hint to the Malays that religion and communism were not compatible'. Communist propaganda distributed to Malay villages 'refrained from criticising or condemning Islam'.[6] Despite these measures, the MCP attracted very little support from the Malay population, and this contributed greatly to their eventual defeat. The presence of a copy of the Koran in a terrorist camp was highly unusual.

That was yesterday - today we heard firing from our ambush party so we hope they've got a kill. They've no wireless set so we shan't know for some time. Searching the area we found their food dump (chillis only) and two cultivations. They made no effort to stand and fight, and as they all seem to be world champion runners, our job is very difficult. We may get some surrenders out of this as their morale must be pretty low.

26 JANUARY 1954, LIPIS

Yes, the ambush party came off - they got a bandit who walked in on the 21st. One less bastard. Shot him clean as a whistle at 30 yards, so I'm very pleased. We had a bottle of champagne on the strength of it last night. The ambush party carried him out on a pole, and we stayed in till last night, and found and destroyed two more cultivations - a good operation.

Illustration 24 in the picture section shows the written orders I had given to the corporal commanding the ambush party, and the corpse of the terrorist they shot. I now don't understand why my men fired at 30 yards as usually shooting in successful ambushes took place at much closer ranges than that. Perhaps the terrorist had heard a noise and turned to run before coming nearer.

Life has been rather hectic lately. At 2.30 p.m. today we killed another three bastards within two miles of our camp at Lipis, including the Lipis bandit leader, a man with $15,000 £1,750 on his head. One of our ambush parties got him, his second in command and one other, at point blank range. I had

to go and bring them in. Not a very pretty sight, but a joy to behold.

This ambush party was led by our CSM. As the three corpses lay stretched out on their backs on the ground with unmarked faces and eyes closed, they looked like dolls rather than men. Something undefinable about their appearance told me at the first glance that they were dead and not asleep, and I did not need the confirmation of seeing the bullet wounds in their torsos which were covered by groundsheets. The illustrations of the numbers of corpses perhaps reveal their feelings at the moment of death – Lim looks angry, Chan exhausted and Sani the Malay looks calm. It was unusual for Chinese and Malay terrorists to operate together, but these men were members of their 12th Regiment, which was a mixed unit.

The Colonel has sent a telegram to Templer so you can tell it's quite good. We'd been after this chap for three months. This was the 23rd ambush we'd set for him. A lot of work, but we got him, and I'd have given a month's pay to have been there. I enclose a few propaganda books, the real McCoy. The written stuff is, believe it or not, a communist Victory Song. Nothing could have been less victorious than their owner when I saw him.

The front page of the *Singapore Standard* newspaper of 28 January 1954 reported this ambush. An extract from the article is shown below:

Lim Men Sek, the English-educated 'Terror of Kuala Lipis', is dead – and according to an official spokesman, there are 'many people in Kuala Lipis, Raub and Bentong who can now sleep more easily.' The terror was fatally shot while running away from a platoon of B Company, the 6th Battalion of the Malay Regiment. He was known to have murdered personally three Malays and to have been concerned in the burning of buses and attacks on the Benta Rubber Estate when the offices were burned. It is now known that about a year ago he went to Kuala Lipis town and attended a cinema show at Chinese New Year. He had a woman companion in the jungle.

Lim belonged to Kuala Lipis; as a boy he attended Clifford School there. He had terrorised the merchants of the town and extorted money from them. Documents concerning these blackmail transactions were found on his body. Lim (a district committee member) and two companions were tracked down in the Kuala Lipis area at 2.30 p.m. yesterday by a section of 4 Platoon, led by Company Sergeant Major Mohd. Yunus. Lim fired three revolver shots on the run. After a 150-yard chase, all three terrorists were killed. With him died Chan Man [sic] Sin, a branch committee member, and bodyguard Sani.'

SINGAPORE TIGER STANDARD

星洲虎報

AIR-EDITION

Vol. IV. No. 210. SINGAPORE, THURSDAY, JANUARY 28, 1954 TWELVE PAGES 10 CENTS.

TERROR OF LIPIS IS DEAD

Blackmailer Falls To Guns Of Malay Regt.

KUALA LUMPUR, Wed.–Lim Meng Sek, the English-educated "Terror of Kuala Lipis" is dead–and according to an official spokesman, there are "many people in the districts of Kuala Lipis, Raub and Bentong who can now sleep more easily."

The terror was fatally shot while running away from a platoon of B Company, the 6th Battalion of the Malay Regiment.

He was known to have murdered personally three Malays and to have been concerned in the burning of buses and attacks on the Benta Rubber Estate when the offices were burned.

It is now known that about a year ago he went to Kuala Lipis town and attended a cinema show at Chinese New Year. He had a woman companion in the jungle.

Lim belonged to Kuala Lipis; as a boy he attended Clifford School there. He had terrorised the merchants of the town and extorted money from them.

Blackmail Papers Found On His Body

Documents concerning these blackmail transactions were found on his body.

Altogether, six terrorists were killed by the security forces yesterday. They were Lim who was a district committee member; two other district committee members; two branch committee members; and Lim's Malay bodyguard, named Sani.

Announcing these kills, the Federation Government said that the "successes resulted from long and careful collection by the Police Force Special Branch of information regarding the movements of Communists and by strict control of food supplies, which forced the terrorists to take risks . . . "

Lim and two companions were tracked down in the Kuala Lipis area at 2.30 p.m. yesterday by a section of 4 Platoon, led by Company Sergeant Major Inche Mohd. Yunus bin Tudi.

Three Killed After 150-Yd. Jungle Chase

Lim fired three revolver shots on the run. After a 150-yard chase, all three terrorists were killed.

With him died Chan Man Sin, a branch committee member and bodyguard Sani

The *Singapore Standard*'s ambush report, 1954.

```
If you'd seen their weapons you'd have no fear for my safety,
old and probably not capable of firing.
```

Some terrorists were still using weapons and ammunition obtained by the MPAJA during the war. In 1955 a terrorist was killed who had been carrying rounds of .303 ammunition some of which were dated 1941.[7] Other terrorists had modern weapons obtained by raiding police stations, home guard posts and ambushing security force convoys. Why a leader as notorious as the 'Terror' carried nothing more than an old revolver was a mystery.

30 JANUARY 1954, LIPIS

```
I went out for a two day operation, no bandits, but quite a
nice food dump.
  Roy Fletcher (a fine OC) and I are probably going as
Gauleiters to a New Village which is giving considerable help
to bandits. Our role will be patrolling, ambushing and put-
ting the fear of God into the co-operating Chinese. It's an
interesting job, and we are already working out schemes for
the discomfiture of the banditry and their supporters (curfew,
house-to-house searches and generally making a ruddy nuisance
```

of ourselves). It will probably be a long job (month or so) stuck in the wilds with no entertainment.

Saw an eight foot long black cobra (hamadryad) the other day. Missed him with my revolver, but the vehicle behind (it was on the road) ran over him.

Yet another attempt to kill something that was doing no harm at the time, though cobras could be highly dangerous if you met them while on foot.

Last operation we caught a scaly ant-eater about two foot long. It has a fantastically powerful tail which it wraps round trees. It can crush a man's arm, and has even been known to kill an elephant by gripping its trunk.

This animal was a Pangolin which is arboreal and has a prehensile tail, but I have not been able to find any confirmation that this creature has ever killed an elephant.[8]

31st I shall not be going to the New Village unfortunately. I (and my platoon) are being left in Lipis with a carte blanche as far as operations go - ambushing etc. Shall be on my own and my own master.

At the moment we have a night ambush out after five visiting a house in Lipis for food - it's the Chinese New Year on the 2nd and we hope to blow the lot into the river. I have armed the boys with repeating 12 bore shotguns and machine guns so it should be quite a party if they turn up.

They did not. Another example of faulty intelligence from the police.

We encourage the boys to wear European dress - white slacks, shirts and reasonable ties. The Malay is very fastidious in dress and some of them put us to shame. We have to correct a regrettable tendency to American ties and yellow shoes occasionally, but they are very much better turned out than the British troops in the area. They hardly ever get drunk and never nasty (no cases since I've been here) - rarely take more than two beers. Only my sergeant drinks rum, and that sparingly. Mind you the Imam (religious fellow) plays hell with me when he comes up, but I put a stop to that by asking how many wives he's divorced (a sore point!).

Simon Pritchard is out of hospital and is Gauleiter of a New Village.

Simon was hospitalised from time to time with a liver problem, probably caused by drinking contaminated stream water in the jungle. The water purification tablets we were issued with gave the water a foul taste, and after trying them once I never used them again, but instead had the stream water boiled and made into tea.

11 FEBRUARY 1954, BENCHAH FOREST

Six day operation finished on the 9th.

I had been briefed for this operation by the Colonel in person, and because there was no large table in our primitive company mess at Lipis he spread his map on the floor and we knelt down to study it while he gave me his orders. He had just laid his finger on a square on the map that he wanted me to reach when Bonzo, his terrier, walked onto the map, causing the Colonel to take his hand away while he pushed him off. When he put his finger back on the map, I was astonished to see he was now pointing at a square which was much nearer Lipis than the first one he had selected. I wondered whether to query this apparent change of plan, but as the trek to the second square he had chosen would take two days less than the trek to the first, I decided to keep quiet. Had I been killed on this operation should Bonzo have been court-martialled? Had we shot ten terrorists should Bonzo have been awarded the Dickin medal (the animal VC)?

Had a phone call from the colonel telling me to stop operations, and 'hold the fort', whatever that means. Whatever it means, I'm ruddy good at holding forts especially when it means not going in the jungle!

The order was given because I was then the only officer present in the company, as illness, leave and courses had removed the others.

17 FEBRUARY 1954, LIPIS

The Colonel seems quite pleased with me, and I believe my stock is fairly high. I try and keep out of trouble and do my best. One advantage of detachment is that we only see the Colonel once a week. He is a 'character', violently rude to all except his own officers (and to them too on occasion) but his bark is twice as bad as his bite, and I pull his leg with impunity:

'Are you worth your pay, Chynoweth?'

'Yes, Sir, if only because I'm grossly underpaid!'
He came up yesterday and ordered me on leave, the sort of visit I appreciate!
'Can't have my officers overworked.'
'Definitely NOT, Sir!'
Captured some bandit propaganda stuff the other day, also some maps - and quite accurate too.
I should like to have some of our MPs and Times letter writers out here to see the atmosphere in a New Village, and to carry a dead bandit five miles through primary jungle. The alternative is unpleasant, but not so exhausting.

This comment followed criticism of the Army in the House of Commons and in the British Press for decapitating dead terrorists for identification purposes, and for displaying the heads in Chinese New Villages to discourage the inhabitants from supporting terrorists. Despite all the steps taken to remove Chinese squatters from communist influence, some New Villagers still continued to support the terrorists.

According to the official list of Army equipment, every platoon should have been issued with a camera to photograph terrorist corpses for identification.[9] Why no cameras were issued to 6 Malay remains a mystery. A body hung on a pole to be carried out of the jungle soon began to decay, and within a few hours the smell was horrible. Decapitation with a parang was sickening. Carrying stinking corpses on poles, or severed heads leaking blood in back packs, was unpopular with the men. Cutting off hands for fingerprinting was the least disgusting method, but was also the least certain way of identifying the dead because Special Branch did not have fingerprint records of all terrorists.

In April 1952 the communist British newspaper the *Daily Worker* had published a photograph of a Royal Marine commando holding the severed head of a terrorist. The Colonial Secretary stated in the House of Commons that in an action a year earlier, a Royal Marine patrol had been ambushed and an officer and an NCO had been killed. One terrorist had been killed and decapitated by a Dyak tracker. The Colonial Secretary said that High Commissioner Templer had been ordered to stop decapitations and to have bodies identified by photographs and fingerprints.[10] This order was ignored by some army units, which took whatever steps were necessary to avoid further criticism.

We once came across the naked corpse of a Chinese male, almost certainly a terrorist who had died of sickness or wounds, caught up in the branches of a tree overhanging a river down which it had been swept. It was enormously swollen and looked like a giant yellow balloon, and I could not resist putting a bullet into its midriff. The body collapsed as the gas rushed out, and we all ran like hell to get away from the terrible stench. No parts of this corpse were brought back for identification purposes!

The civilian Home Guard numbers 250,000, it's compulsory. Armed with shotguns they are a regular source of supply to bandits who attack their posts. The Chinese and Malay Home Guards surrender at the double and hand over all their weapons and ammunition. A big mistake to make it compulsory I feel.

The civilian English do exactly nothing to help win the Emergency. If I was Gauleiter I'd have every one on food checks at the gates, and other ideas I'm not allowed to use - puncturing all their tin cans so nothing can be saved.

This criticism was too generalised. Most English planters and mine managers stayed at their posts despite the risks, and thus contributed greatly to the Malayan economy. Civilians in towns were less praiseworthy. General Templer seems to have agreed with me for once when he criticised the British community in Kuala Lumpur as partygoers who sat back and let others do the work for them.[11]

It's my experience that the less an officer is 'all good form and correct' the better he is. More army business is done on the Old Boy net than any other. If I ring up the adjutant and say: 'Hello Chris you old sod, what about some leave?' I'm much more likely to get it than via a formal application to Captain Christopher Figgens.

21 FEBRUARY 1954, PARAMOUNT HOTEL, PENANG, ON SIX DAYS' LEAVE

I flew down (RAF) to Kuala Lumpur, and caught the night train to Penang. Weather glorious and Penang looking very pretty. Spent yesterday at the Swimming Club, a lovely saltwater pool right by the sea. Have also managed to get a couple of games of tennis.

The present OC is very pleasant and good fun.

24 FEBRUARY 1954, LIPIS

Why some people consider a 'fwightefully' good accent a necessity for a commission I don't know. On this job strong shoulder muscles are much more useful.

It's the informers who get the rewards, another example of the screwy set up out here. It is a civilian's obligation to report bandit activity. Why pay them for what they are obliged by law to do anyway? The reason is clear - expediency - but this is no legal justification.

My criticism of the policy of rewarding informers was wrong. It was essential to get information, and those who gave it risked retribution from terrorist killer squads, and therefore needed to be bribed to take the risk. Unfortunately the prospect of rewards tempted some people to invent information which was inadequately checked by the police, and this resulted in the Army wasting much time on abortive operations.

Another interesting problem is the unofficial encouragement of Aboriginal Sakai to kill bandits with blowpipes (they have already got two). Entirely illegal I should say. Two who killed a British soldier with an axe after encouragement by bandits got life. A very dangerous practice to encourage Aboriginals with the intelligence of a child of ten to go shooting blowpipes at people.

The Sakai were extremely primitive, could count only up to three, and reputedly had minds like young children. They also had some odd taboos, including not laughing in the presence of butterflies which they believed to be the spirits of their departed dead.[12] But see the description of their ingenious sounding device in the letter of 9 December 1953 in Chapter 4.

10 MARCH 1954, SUNGAI TENGGLAM

Roy and I have been on a week's operation. In by helicopter (15 minutes) and out by foot (seven days). No rain for ages here and rivers drying up makes it difficult to camp as we must have water. Going in by helicopter we were able to take in some beer. Very nice on returning from a patrol to have a pint that's been cooling in a stream. We did over 30,000 yards 17 miles - a lot in the jungle. One of our patrols was fired on, but no other excitement.

Not strictly true. Roy Fletcher's need for whisky resulted in a worrying incident at breakfast one morning towards the end of the operation, when his batman threw away the last remaining Scotch which Roy, before going into the bushes to relieve himself, had poured into the remnants of his coffee and which the batman had assumed to be dregs. Livid with rage, Roy pulled out his revolver and ordered him to run to the nearest village to buy a bottle of whisky. I reminded Roy that the nearest village was two days' march away, and was most unlikely to have Scotch. I suggested that instead we should end the operation forthwith as we had run out of essential supplies, hurry to the nearest road, stop the first passing vehicle, and drive to the first village which had a bar. This we did. Provided Scotch was available, Roy was always good-tempered. When we lay in our tent each evening he used to say: 'You pour my drink, John, you always give me more than I would give myself.' This was not strictly true either!'

Enclosed is a book of communist songs found in a food dump on this operation. To cheer the comrades round the camp fire in the evening.

13 MARCH 1954, LIPIS

Our company moves to Triang in south Pahang on 2 April. Battalion HQ is to be at Mentakab some 60 miles from Triang.

Mentakab is only about twenty miles from Triang, though the laterite road between the two was so hot and dusty it felt more like the sixty miles I had wrongly reported.

We have a new Malay 2nd Lieutenant (Othman) straight from Cadet School, seems OK.

Malayanisation had long been underway, and 6 Malay would eventually become the first of the Regiment's battalions to be completely officered by Malays.

On the 18th there is a battalion operation, a final fling against the local banditry. Our task involves a 15 mile march and will take about ten days. Needless to say yours truly is not frightfully thrilled. And on arrival at Triang we are going straight out on an operation to impress the locals!

At around this time, I had a nasty shock when I was called to the company office and found myself faced with an Army team investigating fraud. Often when I returned to camp after operations, our Malay CQMS, who was responsible for arranging with outside contractors to supply services such as laundering the troops' uniforms, would ask me to sign chits authorising him to pay their bills. Usually exhausted and well into my third large brandy and ginger ale, and never doubting the honesty of such a long serving warrant officer, I always signed the chits without studying the details.

The investigating team handed me a pile of chits which, they said, were all fraudulent, and invited me to look at the authorising signatures. As I worked through them I was appalled to see that all the signatures were mine, and my heart sank as I expected to be accused of having come to some arrangement with the CQMS. Just as despair began to set in I found, near the bottom of the pile, several chits with Roy's signature on them. What relief! Of course I got a severe telling off for not checking, but no other punishment. We later discovered that the CQMS had got into debt through spending too much money in the houseboat brothels on the river at Lipis while trying to maintain two wives at home in his village.

23 MARCH 1954, KAMPONG TANJONG BESAR

Just returned from an operation, only four days, but we covered 24,000 yards in a straight line including two hills of over 1,000 feet.

This trek of thirteen and a half miles averaged just under three and a half miles per day, or about half a mile an hour, which was quite fast going for operations in hilly primary jungle. In emergencies, such as running out of food (or alcohol!) after failing to receive an airdrop, greater distances could be achieved for a day or two.

No bandit activity, but an interesting map-reading experience, four days on one compass bearing. We finally arrived only 400 yards from where we'd aimed for. Each evening at about 4.00 p.m. there was a thunderstorm, torrential rain heralded by about two minutes of howling wind. This two minutes gave us enough warning to rush to a bit of flat ground and put up our tents. Each man on his own, and the Tuan wielding his parang with the best of them! A storm in the jungle is quite an experience. Pitch black, sheets of rain, thunder and lightning, high wind, trees creaking. In one of these storms two days ago a tree fell on three African troops, killing one and seriously injuring the others, bad luck and quite rare.

When Osman China, who was in charge of communist propaganda, surrendered in 1954 it was learned that his left leg had once been broken by a tree falling in a storm and was now two inches shorter than his right.[13]

Off again tomorrow (how I earn my 17s 6d per day!).

This understated my income as I was then receiving 13*s* National Service pay, 4*s* 6*d* regular increment, 4s Malay Regiment pay, and 9*s* local overseas allowance, less 8*d* income tax, net total 29*s* 10*d* (£1.49) per day. This was just enough for me to live on as I spent no money while in the jungle. What infuriated me was that each month I received a Brigade mess bill, which included my share of the cost of entertaining guests, though I was nearly always out on operations while they were being wined and dined by the resident staff officers, who never went near the jungle.

Unlike my colleagues, I did not have the pay of a regular, or a private income, or financial help from home. My lack of money meant I was unable to take advantage of my location by spending my leaves visiting Hong Kong and Bangkok. How I now regret inheriting the Victorian contempt felt by my parents for people who borrowed money!

This time in by helicopter after a bandit cultivation. Have got a whacking great bottle of rum to keep the rain out.

I've received the General Service Medal ('Malaya' clasp) inscribed with my name, but as a cook in Singapore also gets it, it means nothing.

The issue of campaign medals to servicemen who were never exposed to danger always annoyed the infantry.

I met an Aboriginal the other day, and asked him why the Sakai always ran away when a helicopter landed. He said they were afraid the men in them would capture their food. When I pointed out that their food consisted of snakes and tortoises, he said: 'Ah, but it's the eggs you are after!'

This man offered to guide us to a terrorist camp in return for a cigarette. I asked how long it would take to get there and he said we would arrive as he finished his smoke. Delighted with the shortness of the march which lay ahead we set off, but I soon became suspicious as after a couple of puffs our guide pinched out his cigarette and put it behind his ear. This happened more than once, and several hours later he took his final drag, dropped the butt, pointed ahead, and disappeared into the bushes. The camp, of course, proved to be old and empty.

29 MARCH 1954, LIPIS

We didn't go on the operation after all as the helicopters couldn't land us. They took me to the clearing and hovered at 20 feet, but couldn't risk going lower as the clearing was too small.

11 APRIL 1954, SUNGAI MENGKUANG

We returned from the operation last night having been out a week. An absolutely dead area, no signs of bandits more recent than six months old. The jungle here is flat - few hills of more than 200 feet, but plenty of swamp and, of course, leeches. Water is stagnant and bad, and it's damned hot.

This was my last operation though I did not know it at the time. After a few days we came across a square grave, built above ground and made of interlocking planks of wood. It was about 4ft high with the contents topped with gravel. My sergeant said it was not the grave of a member of any race native to Malaya, and I wondered whether it might be that of Pat Noone. I wanted to open it to see if I could solve the mystery of his disappearance, but was persuaded not to because my men were afraid of ghosts. The account of Noone's life and death given in the Epilogue explains the true circumstances of his disappearance, but the mystery of this strange grave remains unsolved.

20 APRIL 1954, OFFICERS' MESS, 2 KING'S AFRICAN RIFLES, KUANTAN, ON SIX DAYS' LEAVE

Arrived by air on Saturday. Kuantan has a magnificent beach, swimming is lovely. On Sunday I went pig shooting - saw one, but too far away to get a shot. The African troops seem nice fellows, black as ink, and a lot bigger than the Malays. Their idea of a smart civilian outfit consists of anything with clashing colours. I saw a very smart sergeant in a pair of black tails and a tartan shirt!

24 APRIL 1954, TRIANG

I borrowed a gramophone to play some Malay records I've bought only to find they've bent in the heat. It's impossible to keep any damn thing in this climate. Clothes ruined by careless dhobi, damp gets into cameras, all metal things rust, ants eat books, fungus grows on photos, and now my records melt!

When I left England for Malaya, my father gave me a canvas valise which had accompanied him, without damage, for three years in trenches in France and Italy during the First World War. On my first night in Lipis, I left it on the earthen floor of my bedroom and a column of ants arrived and ate it to pieces. Needless to say, I failed to report this in my letters home. While I was at Triang, Roy Fletcher invited me to dinner in his married quarter in Mentakab. The drive up the laterite road was dusty and hot, so when I arrived I asked if I might shower before dinner. While I was in the shower the curtain parted and a hand passed in a large tumbler filled with clear liquid. I foolishly assumed it was a cold soft drink and downed it gratefully. When I fell over a few minutes later I realised it had been one of Roy's 'specials' – 95 per cent gin and 5 per cent tonic. When I sat down for dinner and looked at Roy's wife, I could see two of her sitting side by side, and I realised that disaster lay ahead. I rose unsteadily, pleaded the sudden onset of a fever, apologised profusely, and headed for the door.

3 MAY 1954, TEMERLOH, RETRAINING

We left Triang on Sunday for Temerloh, both small towns, couple of rows of shops, no cinemas, no amusements, and damned hot. We started retraining today - no rest cure with bags of parades, drill, PT, firing, etc. Each move is very tiring, 150 men plus kit to pack up. All the roads here are red laterite and very dusty, with a convoy visibility reduced to 20 yards. Everyone arrives hot, tired, and filthy.

8 MAY 1954, TEMERLOH, RETRAINING

I've bought a smart blue HMV gramophone, and having straightened my records under a pile of bricks, am rendering the evening hideous with noise.

During retraining I had a brilliant idea for how to practise firing the grenade-throwing rifle without using live grenades. Practising with this dangerous weapon was essential – as is explained in the notes to my letter of 10 July 1953 in Chapter 3. I had noticed that a cylindrical tin of fifty Players cigarettes was the same size as a grenade, and if filled with sand, would be about the same weight. I put up this idea at an officers' meeting, where I was congratulated on my inventiveness.

The RSM was ordered to arrange for every empty tin to be saved, filled with sand and have the lid taped on. As nearly all soldiers smoked cigarettes in those days, plenty of tins were available, and when 100 had been assembled we gathered on the parade ground for a demonstration. The RSM picked up a tin to fire the first 'grenade', but could not get it into the cup on the muzzle of the rifle – it was a fraction of an inch too wide! Admiration for the brilliance of my idea vanished.

13 MAY 1954, TEMERLOH, RETRAINING

The GOC Malaya (Lieutenant General Bourne) and entourage graced our mess for lunch yesterday, and caused a considerable flap.

The flap was caused by the late arrival of the roast chickens which had been ordered from a local Chinese restaurant, which had that morning suffered a problem with its ovens. The delay meant that the pre-lunch trays of champagne had circulated so many times before we finally sat down that several present had difficulty in focussing on their plates. This was not the only military luncheon for distinguished guests which encountered delivery problems with its food. In 1942, when Prime Minister Churchill was visiting the 8th Army at El Alamein, he was invited to lunch with the senior RAF officers, who had ordered special delicacies from Shepheard's Hotel in Cairo. The car bringing the food got lost, and despite frantic efforts to find it, arrived late.[14]

The General is quite nice, one arm, rows of ribbons, and a piercing stare. Last night we had a regimental dinner in his honour, plus the regimental band. Only had a few hours sleep, was up at 5.00 a.m. to go to the range.

19 MAY 1954, MENTAKAB, RETRAINING

Following the defeat of the French at Dien Bien Phu on 7 May 1954 there was concern that the Vietnamese communists might invade Siam en route to Malaya.

Probably some of the Malay Regiment battalions would be the first to line the frontier though I don't think it's a

possibility yet. The natural frontier runs through Siam. I should think the thing to do is to copy the Reds, 'liberate' south Siam, and defend the neck of land, but only if the Reds invaded Siam first.

Just north of the western end of the border between Malaya and Siam the land narrows to a width of about 50 miles and this was the only place where a land attack on Malaya from the north had a chance of being stopped. A Vietnamese invasion of Malaya never happened, and communist supporters have exaggerated the effect that the Dien Bien Phu defeat had on the colonial powers. The head of the Centre for Khmer Studies in Cambodia has recently claimed that: 'The white man's prestige was shattered by the small colonised man'. This may have been true of the French, but it certainly did not apply to the British whose Army led the defeat of Malayan communism.[15]

One has to supervise Malay NCOs more than British, and the Colonel is mad keen on getting a good battalion, therefore we work!

During my stay at Mentakab, I heard a tragic story about one of our officers. Captain Eric Barter had recently been court-martialled and dismissed from the Army for being drunk while planning an operation which resulted in one of our platoons exchanging fire across a river with a platoon of Gurkhas. Despite claims of kills by both sides, nobody was hurt. I was given Barter's old bedroom at camp, and while putting my clothes in the chest of drawers, I found his Military Cross lying under a pile of old socks. I could not believe that anyone would have abandoned such a decoration, and began to enquire into his background.

I learned that while he was on leave in England the previous year he had got engaged, and when he returned to Malaya he told his brother Frank, who was a captain in 5 Malay, to go and meet his fiancée when he next went home on leave. Frank did so, the girl fell for him, and sent him a love letter when he returned to Malaya. An Army postal clerk misread her '5' as '6', and Eric, not noticing that the initial on the envelope was 'F' not 'E', opened the letter. The loss of his fiancée, and the end of his friendship with his brother, proved too much, and he hit the bottle. On leaving the Army he joined the South African Police, but committed suicide not long afterwards.

Roy Fletcher had a minor but unusual problem while at Mentakab. He was standing in his bath one night when he slipped, fell on his bottom and his legs shot forward and upwards so that a big toe rammed itself up the hot tap and became wedged. The battalion medical officer was summoned and pulled his toe out though all the skin was left behind. Bandaged up, Roy retired to bed. The following day, the Colonel, who had not heard of the accident, ordered Roy out on a week's jungle operation as a punishment for getting drunk and misbehaving during a mess night a few days earlier.

Roy refused to plead incapacity, and sent his batman to fetch one of the square metal tins in which the troops' rice was packed when airdropped. Having had the top of the tin cut off with a tin opener and the rice tipped out, Roy eased in his bandaged foot which was well padded with a towel, and had the tin and his leg strapped together. He then hobbled to his jeep with his batman carrying a pack heavy with bottles, and departed for the jungle escorted by one of our platoons. I was later told by the accompanying sergeant that Roy had camped in a clearing a few yards in from the jungle edge, had a nice shelter built with a comfortable bed of cut ferns, and spent his days sunbathing and his nights sampling the contents of the bottles. He sent sections of the escort to search the area around the camp and they found and destroyed several food dumps and cultivations, results which pleased the Colonel. The medical officer said that Roy was lucky to have escaped gangrene, but I believed that the level of alcohol in his bloodstream killed all known germs.

28 MAY 1954, SEGINTING RANGE, PORT DICKSON, RETRAINING

We are in the middle of ten days firing on the ranges here by the sea. We fire from 7.00 a.m. till [hole in letter, probably 9.00 a.m.], and from 4.00 p.m. till 6.00 p.m.

The Army did not supply ear protectors in those days and standing close to Bren guns while they were being fired gave me tinnitus. Our medical officer wrongly diagnosed my problem as 'Singapore ear' (a fungal infection), and poured neat iodine into each orifice – ouch!

Another delightful experience at Seginting was having to crawl out into the scrub to place slabs of gun cotton with detonators alongside those grenades which had been thrown but which had failed to explode. One of the slabs I took out also failed to explode so a second visit became necessary. As I crawled back towards safety, I thought about what an exploding grenade and two exploding slabs of gun cotton might do to my backside.

30 MAY 1954, SEGINTING RANGE, PORT DICKSON, RETRAINING

I have been chosen to represent the battalion at the Queen's Birthday Parade in Kuala Lumpur on the 10 June. Each bat-

talion in Malaya is sending one officer and 20 men. Quite an honour to be chosen, but I hate drill. I have to learn sword drill too. I hope I don't drop the sword on the parade! We go to Kuala Lumpur on the 3rd for a week's practising. I'm not looking forward to this part of it. I'd much rather watch parades than take part in them.

The Colonel gave me a lesson in sword drill for an hour or two one evening. When he first tried to draw his sword he failed, because it had corroded into its scabbard – typical of the tropical climate's effect on equipment.

2 JUNE 1954, STATION HOTEL, KUALA LUMPUR, PRACTICE PARADES

Am putting up at Army's expense at the Station Hotel, big and comfortable. Practice parades beginning tomorrow, but the afternoon and evening off.

Our adjutant had forgotten to book accommodation for me until the day before I was due to arrive in Kuala Lumpur, and all he could find that was available was the bridal suite at this hotel, which was then one of the city's finest. I enjoyed the suite even though it lacked a bride. The hotel was still in business in 2003, though at nothing like the standard of 1954.

16 JUNE 1954, MENTAKAB, RETRAINING

The Kuala Lumpur parade went off OK, and we've had a signal of congratulation from the parade commander. Congratulatory signals were received from His Excellency and the GOC.

I never understood why these signals were sent because the parade was marred by numerous cock-ups. The rehearsals had taken place outside Kuala Lumpur so the parade commander had not noticed that there was a clock tower behind him at the parade ground. At 8.00 a.m. on the day of the Queen's Birthday, he began to give the order for a Royal Salute just as the clock gave the first chime. 'Parade!' DONG. Half the contingents failed to hear the remainder of the order so did not present arms. The officer commanding the Planter Volunteer contingent standing next to mine wore an unusual Sam Browne belt with bulging leather pouches on the strap across his chest, rather like a bus conductor's equipment. As we began to march towards the reviewing stand, he said loudly: 'Ting, ting, fares please', which made me double up with laughter. The speed of marching of the units varied so considerably that during the march past the stand the contingent representing the Light Infantry, which was marching at 140 paces to the minute, was treading on the heels of the contingent in front of them, which was marching at 120 paces to the minute, as was the contingent behind them, which was being left in the middle distance. When saluting the dignitaries on the stand, I lowered the point of my sword a little too far so it dug into the turf, causing a hiccup in my stride. After the parade all officers were ordered to report to HQ Malaya that evening, but suspecting that it was to receive a rocket, I returned to Mentakab forthwith. On reading the telegrams, it looked as if I had missed not a rocket but a celebratory drinks party!

During my return to Malaya in 2003, I visited the parade ground which is in front of the old colonial government buildings. I studied the turf to find the hole I had made with the point of my sword, but curiously enough it seemed to have gone.

30 JUNE 1954, MENTAKAB, END OF RETRAINING

Tonight we go to a dance in the sergeants' mess, tomorrow to a dinner night, on Friday to an end of retraining party with hired dancing girls (at vast expense from Siam) on Saturday move to Triang, and on Sunday in the jungle - quite a rush.

The Colonel has just put me up for a mention in despatches, quite what for I don't know.

GHQ did not know either, for no such award was forthcoming.

This incidentally is for your private ear alone.

4 JULY 1954, TRIANG CAMP

I've not gone into the jungle. It is going to be a three week operation and it was reckoned I'd done my bit. I'm in charge of this huge (400 man) camp, and given 30 men to guard it, no water, no food, no electricity, and lots of valuable army property to guard. This is written by four candle power so excuse writing.

I said goodbye to my platoon at a party they gave for me, bags of hot curry and speeches. I made my reply in Malay - a test of nerve if ever there was one. They presented me with a complete Malay ceremonial costume (satin trousers and jacket, silver embroidered sarong, and black songkok) which, needless to say, rather overwhelmed me. I wasn't awfully dry eyed when all this was over.

8th Last night I went to a Chinese feast to celebrate one of the merchants being made a JP. A continuous relay of dishes from 8.30 p.m. till midnight, and bags of brandy. The excitement was too much for one merchant who had a heart attack and died, and was carried out in his chair. As the evening went on others were carried out for another reason. The Chinese habit of saying 'Yam sing' (bottoms up) just after your glass has been refilled makes these parties pretty rugged.

The dead merchant in his chair was placed at the foot of the stairs awaiting removal to the morgue, and on our way out at the end of the party, we all shook his hand and thanked him for his hospitality. I was so drunk that as I tottered past the guardroom back at camp I swayed into a pyramid of fire buckets and brought the whole lot crashing down. The guard rushed out to shoot the interloper, but fortunately recognised the Tuan in time.

The other day I saw a huge five foot monitor lizard on the road here, like a small crocodile, but quite harmless.

While in charge of Triang camp I was told that a general would be calling in during the following week en route to the north. At the time the camp latrines were smelling badly, and I could get no quick lime with which to treat them. There were some drums of petrol in a hut in the camp, so I had them poured into the latrines followed by a lighted brand; the resulting explosion cured the problem and made the camp fit to receive the visitor. When the general's helicopter landed the pilot asked me where the drums of aviaton gasolene for refuelling were stored. Trying to look puzzled I said I knew of none. A furious general had to use my jeep for his journey north along the hot and dusty laterite road. My encounters with generals seldom seemed to have gone well.

19 JULY 1954, MALAY REGIMENT DEPOT, PORT DICKSON, EMBARKATION LEAVE

Well, we've made it at last! Simon and I arrived here this afternoon from Mentakab after a series of very touching farewells, most of which were well lubricated. All set for ten days bathing and lazing.

23 JULY 1954, PORT DICKSON

Was glad not to have had to do any more operations, my imagination grew more vivid as my demobilisation grew nearer! On the last operation that I might have done the company got two bandits, one by my platoon, though in ambush so I would have been as safe as houses.

Life is very pleasant here, swimming every day, game of billiards, breakfast in bed, but we are really time killing - to get home is what we want!

On 1 August, Simon and I took the train to Singapore, spent a night in the Raffles Hotel and then flew to Heathrow the following day, arriving on 3 August.

*

The operations described in this and the previous two chapters varied in length from one or two days or nights of static ambushes to one or two weeks of jungle treks with airdrops of food every four or five days. Though the operations all took place within a 500 square-mile rectangle of Pahang, the conditions we encountered varied greatly. Some primary jungle was flat, relatively cool and free from undergrowth, so movement was not unlike a walk through an English wood on a hot summer's day, though it was made tiring by 70lb of pack plus a gun. Mountainous primary jungle involved climbing cliffs by hauling oneself up on bushes and creepers, and spending nights above 3,000ft awake and shivering in the cold air. Traversing secondary jungle was a nightmare because creepers, bushes, thorns and thickets of bamboo required hacking with parangs to get through, and the lack of a tree canopy allowed the sun to beat down and exhaust everyone in no time. Swamps were always unpleasant, with stinking water, abundant leeches and the possibility of treading in an elephant footprint and sinking below the surface. Insect life varied from large pretty butterflies to tiny biting sand-flies which left us with swollen itching faces.

Nearly all the information about terrorist activity supplied by the police to my company proved to be useless, and if my comments seem to be unduly critical of that organisation, then readers might like to read a book written by a police lieutenant who was engaged in jungle operations from 1952 to 1957. Among the numerous problems he encountered with his superiors, the worst occurred when he was sent to carry out an ambush in 1956. When he and his squad arrived at the site he saw a man he assumed to be a terrorist. He was about to shoot him, but instead decided to capture him. The man turned out to be a member of another police squad which had been sent to ambush exactly the same site. Shades of the operation I recorded in my letter of 12 October 1953 in Chapter 4.[16]

Levels of fitness and health began to decline after a week or so in the jungle because of lack of vitamins in the rations, absence of sunlight, clothes perpetually wet through rain and sweat, and insect and leech bites which caused lesions and infections in the skin. Apart from the physical strain of the marches, there was also the mental strain of trying to keep alert in case of ambush.

The results of my operations can be summarised as follows. I was with my company when we shot and killed a terrorist. I set an ambush with a section of my platoon which shot and killed a terrorist. My platoon shot and killed a terrorist in an ambush while I was on leave. A company operation in which I took part resulted in four terrorists surrendering. I fired at, but missed, a terrorist who was running away from a camp which we were attacking. My platoon and I found and destroyed five food dumps, five cultivations and about eight terrorist camps, all except one of which had been vacated but which, if they had not been burned, might have been reoccupied in future. These results seem unimpressive considering I spent 115 days in the jungle, but after talking to other veterans and reading the accounts of their experiences, I learned that my results were fairly typical of those achieved by infantry subalterns at the time.

My operations formed, of course, only a tiny fraction of the whole security force campaign against the terrorists which included the efforts of several hundred other infantry platoons. The following table presents an overall picture of the results of both sides' efforts to destroy each other during 1954. The total number of terrorists 'eliminated' shown in the table included all those who were permanently removed from the conflict as a result of death, capture or surrender. Deaths included those killed by the security forces and those estimated to have died of wounds, sickness, starvation, or execution by their own side.[17]

Terrorists	1954
Number in the jungle	*c.*6,000
Number killed	723
Number captured	51
Number surrendered	211
Number died of wounds, say 25 per cent of the 212 wounded *	53
Number died of sickness, starvation, or execution by their own side, say 5 per cent of the total *	300
TOTAL NUMBER OF TERRORISTS ELIMINATED	1,338
Security forces	
Police killed	53
Police wounded	89

Army killed	34
Army wounded	65
TOTAL SECURITY FORCE CASUALTIES	241
Civilians	
Killed	97
Wounded	31
Missing	57
TOTAL CIVILIAN CASUALTIES	185[18]

* Present author's estimates

The monthly averages were:	
Terrorists eliminated	112
Security force casualties	20
Civilian casualties	15

These figures show the extent to which the terrorists were losing the fight.

Notes

1 Royle, p.62.
2 Miller, *Jungle*, pp.85, 94.
3 Miller, *Menace*, p.51.
4 Robinson, p.171.
5 Ibid., footnote to pp.163-64.
6 A. Chin, pp.40-41.
7 Miers, p.174.
8 *Animal Life*, p.519.
9 ATOM, p.7 e.
10 Chin Peng, pp.302-04.
11 Short, p.342.
12 Ibid., p.452, footnote 10.
13 Robinson, p.155.
14 Churchill, Vol.4, p.377.
15 *The Daily Telegraph*, 8 May 2004, p.17.
16 Follows, pp.90-1, 120-21.
17 In one State in 1951 and 1952, twenty-three terrorists were executed by their own side for being potential deserters or suspected spies; Short, p.421.
18 Ibid., pp.350, 507.

CHAPTER 6

CAMPAIGN ERRORS 1948–54

No military campaign is ever free from error, but in many cases the mistakes are caused by the failure of High Commands to listen to the reports of junior officers about the conditions they were facing in the field, and this results in problems and sometimes disasters. By the summer of 1916, experience had showed that British attacks on the Western Front in France could only obtain some initial success when our preliminary artillery bombardments achieved three objectives. They had to cut through the barbed wire defending the German trenches, crush the entrances to their deep dugouts to prevent the machine gunners sheltering inside from emerging when the bombardment stopped, and destroy their artillery behind the lines. Each night during our bombardments, patrols led by junior officers went into No-Man's Land to assess the extent to which the enemy wire had been cut and whether their defences were being destroyed. During the day, pilots and observers of the Royal Flying Corps flew over the German lines to inspect the results of the bombardments, and to take photographs. Often, the patrol leaders and the aircrews reported that much of the enemy wire, trenches, dugouts and gun batteries were still intact, but these reports were often ignored or disbelieved by the commanding generals.[1] As a result, the attacks went ahead on the pre-arranged dates, and many of the advancing British infantry became trapped in undestroyed wire, mown down by machine guns and blown up by shells. The worst of these disasters occurred on 1 July 1916, the first day of the Battle of the Somme, when British casualties totalled nearly 57,000, of whom more than 19,000 were killed. The High Command should have listened to the reports from the front and delayed the attack until the artillery had achieved the results which were essential for success. It later became known hat about one third of all shells we fired were duds. Field Marshal Sir Douglas Haig, the C-in-C, eventually conceded that, 'this is really a platoon commanders' war', but the diary entry which records his belated conclusion was not made until 29 July 1918, more than two years after the first day of the battle of the Somme and less than four months before the end of the war.[2] Why had it taken so long to recognise this crucial fact?

If the generals in Malaya had listened to the infantry subalterns during the Emergency, they would have learned that deploying platoons to search the jungle for enemy camps without accurate information was nearly always a waste of time. It was like looking for the proverbial needle (which does not move) in the proverbial haystack, and on the few occasions when one was found, the terrorist sentries, who were positioned some way away from their camp, would fire to warn their comrades, who would disperse in a matter of seconds and rendezvous later at some pre-arranged place. Follow-ups rarely succeeded in catching them because men running for their lives run faster than pursuers who are not sure which way their prey has gone, and who need to take care to avoid being ambushed during the chase. This 'jungle bashing' involved millions of infantry man-hours in difficult terrain and tropical temperatures.

The attitude of some senior Army officers in Malaya seems to have been remarkably similar to that of their counterparts in France in 1914–1918. Generals who had just arrived in the country were reportedly often shaken to find that the fighting had 'degenerated' [sic] into a 'subaltern's war'. Shortly after his arrival, General Stockwell expressed his horror at an operation which he thought was 'out of control', because the commanding officer of the battalion concerned had only a vague idea where his platoons were, and had not heard from any of them for four days.[3] Unless 6 Malay's subalterns had some contact or emergency to report, while on operations they remained out of touch with battalion HQ until they required an airdrop of food after four or five days. Even when contact with base was needed, it sometimes could not be made when wireless sets broke down, or if the terrain or weather prevented reception or transmission.

Some senior officers thought that jungle warfare would prove to be easy. General Wade, GOC Malaya for the first few weeks of the Emergency, believed that 'organised drives' would achieve great and satisfactory results in a short time.[4] Many organised drives took place thereafter, but the Emergency lasted for twelve years, or twice as long as the Second World War. His successor, Major-General Boucher, said that, 'this is by far the easiest problem I have ever tackled', but a few months later he returned to England a sick man, and died shortly afterwards.[5]

When General Templer arrived in 1952, he said that given the support of the entire population he could lick the Emergency in three months.[6] For him to have made such a statement was ridiculous, as he knew that there was not the slightest chance of securing this level of support because many Malayan Chinese, who formed about 40 per cent of the total population, disliked the British and the Malays, and supported the terrorists who were nearly all of their own race.

Some generals who had no experience of jungle warfare spent very little time in the Malayan jungle. The biography of Major-General Urquhart,

GOC from 1950 to 1952, mentions only the four hours he spent on a patrol with some Gurkhas in an area containing no mountains or swamps, and which had previously been searched to ensure that no terrorists were present during his visit. Urquhart thought this was 'a very exhausting exercise'.[7] According to his official biographer Templer spent only one night and half a day in the jungle during his two-year reign.[8] These professional soldiers should surely have devoted a little more time to personally assessing the problems facing their troops and taking the appropriate action.

Every general started his military career as a junior officer and will have formed his own conclusions about the conduct of the various campaigns in which he took part. No doubt they sometimes wished their superiors had consulted them about their experiences, so when they themselves became generals, why did they not consult the junior officers under their command? The answer may be the lack of relevant experience available at the start of these campaigns. In 1914 no British officer had previously taken part in trench warfare, and in 1948 no British officer had previously hunted terrorists in the jungle of Malaya, so there were no experienced subordinates available for the generals to consult. Two years later, of course, there were plenty of such people, but by then the generals had formed their own opinions of what needed to be done and how it should be tackled.

There was an alternative strategy to 'jungle bashing' available, namely a much greater use of ambushes. Each army platoon of, say, thirty men, instead of trekking through the jungle as a single unit, could have been divided into three parties of ten men each, armed with a Bren, rifles, shotguns, Stens and grenades. Each party could have spent at least four or five days ambushing a track leading to a likely source of terrorist supplies, and this would have placed the terrorists at risk of encountering three death-traps for every army platoon deployed, instead of only one. The movement of terrorists and Min Yuen through the jungle would have become three times more hazardous, and their morale would have suffered as losses and fears of being ambushed rose sharply. Surrenders as well as kills would have increased. Movement through the jungle was essential for the terrorists as without it they could make no attacks, and could receive no orders from their high command, or supplies or information from the Min Yuen.

The superior effectiveness of ambushing compared with 'jungle bashing' was demonstrated by estimates made during the Emergency. The average time a soldier spent on patrol before seeing a terrorist was estimated to be 1,000 hours, compared with an average of 300 hours spent when ambushing.[9] Thus the expectation of a threefold improvement in kills from deploying platoons in three ambushes was supported by the threefold improvement in contacts, as the chances of achieving kills in ambushes was much higher than the chances of achieving kills following encounters with terrorist sentries guarding camps whose exact location was usually unknown to the army patrol. After the first few years of the Emergency, shortage of food forced most terrorists to operate in small groups of five or six men so the risk of ambush parties of ten well-armed troops being successfully attacked by much larger groups of terrorists was small, especially if the ambush positions chosen could be readily defended. At least one in three of these ambush parties could have been supplied with a wireless set to use in case of emergency, and if a policy of ambushing had been adopted, the number of available sets and signallers could no doubt have been increased.

Ambushing, of course, was not problem-free. An ideal ambush required all the troops involved to maintain absolute silence, and those on watch to keep wide awake and alert. Chatting, smoking, cooking, slapping mosquitoes and burning off leeches with cigarettes were all forbidden. Keeping awake while lying down in tropical temperatures and watching empty tracks for hours was not easy. Boredom rapidly set in, and when terrorists did appear the resulting surprise sometimes caused premature firing and the escape of most of the enemy party. Though involving much less physical effort than 'jungle bashing', ambushing was not always popular with troops because of the problems listed above. Nevertheless, achieving the better results which this policy would have produced was more important than the problems encountered by the troops involved, which perhaps could have been recognised by the granting of improved arrangements for leave.

As the conflict was not officially designated a war, the Army's role was defined as aiding the civil power, and this theoretically placed all its units under the control of the police. The incompetence of successive Chiefs of Police, and the poor quality of many of their senior men, meant that the information about terrorist activities which they supplied to the Army was frequently wrong. Whenever information proved to have been worthless, an enquiry should have been held to establish why this was so, and those responsible for inadequate checking and interrogation of informers should have been suitably disciplined. Although reports of every jungle operation which failed through faulty information were submitted by the platoon commanders concerned, my colleagues and I never received any feedback about what investigation into the reasons why the information was faulty, if any, had been carried out. This poor-quality information, coupled with the Army High Command's failure to properly assess the conditions on the ground, led to continual 'jungle bashing' by large numbers of troops, the results of which bore no relation to the massive efforts involved. An example of this is an operation in June 1953, when three battalions searched for the communist leader who, according to the information supplied to the Army by the police, was camped near the Sungai Liang River. Nearly half a million man-hours were wasted by the 2,000 or so soldiers involved, who spent ten days trekking through the jungle in pursuit of a man who had moved out of the area months before.[10]

By 1954, the Emergency had already lasted as long as the Second World War, but there were still a number of deficiencies in the supplies and equipment available to my battalion and to many others:

1 The food airdropped into the jungle to the British officers consisted solely of twenty-four-hour ration packs, which were not designed for use for more than a few days. They contained no fresh fruit, vegetables or vitamin pills, so they failed to supply certain ingredients essential for good health.
2 No cameras were supplied for taking photographs of dead terrorists for identification purposes, leaving only the unpleasant or unsatisfactory alternatives of corpse-carrying on poles, decapitation or the removal of hands.
3 The available helicopters had very limited carrying capacity, thus necessitating numerous trips to move a platoon into the jungle, and the resulting din from their engines alerted terrorists to military operations in their area.
4 Our wireless sets were bulky and heavy, and frequently failed to send or receive.

Complaints were made about these shortcomings at meetings of the battalion's officers, but nothing was done about them during my time in Malaya. Reports of inadequate Army equipment still regularly appear today. One recent example concerns the portable radios, which are the modern equivalent of the 'wireless sets' I complained about fifty years ago in point 4 above:

> The Army's new £1.9 billion communications system is facing such serious problems that the Director of Infantry initially refused to accept the portable radio into service. Brig. Jamie Balfour was ordered to take the radio 'for political reasons' despite a series of issues that made it 'totally unsuitable' for use in front-line infantry operations.[11]

I think it is only fair that my criticism of the Army's High Command should be accompanied by some criticism of my own performance. Looking back, I am now certain that I should have spent more time training my men to move quietly through the jungle with eyes and ears alert to try to detect signs of the presence of terrorists. It was, of course, impossible for a column of forty men laden with heavy packs, weapons and equipment to constantly move silently through dense vegetation in difficult terrain, but I should also have moved more slowly so as to reduce the level of noise and thus improve our chances of achieving encounters.

We should also have moved more slowly so as to reduce the noise. We moved too quickly because early on the Colonel had said that he was impressed by my speed of movement through the jungle and as this was my only above-average military talent I was determined to maintain this reputation. An example of our speed is recorded in my letter of 23 July 1954 when we had moved 13½ miles in hilly primary jungle in four days, averaging just under 3½ miles per day. This was far too fast for silent movement.

Notes

1 Neillands, *The Great War Generals*, p.241; Middlebrook, pp.92, 98.
2 Terraine, pp.45, 118.
3 Cloake, p.243.
4 Short, p.136.
5 Miller, *Menace*, pp.92-93.
6 Short, p.337.
7 Baynes, p.203.
8 Cloake, p.242.
9 Short, p.481.
10 See my letter of 13 June 1953, in Chapter 3.
11 *Daily Telegraph*, 4 January 2005, p.8. The article details the radio's shortcomings.

CHAPTER 7

The End of the Emergency and an Assessment of Chin Peng

The End of the Emergency

Early in 1953, Chin Peng and his senior comrades had left their camp in Pahang and set up a base in southern Siam, from where they could continue to control the insurrection. They were soon joined by an increasing number of their armed units as the pressure exerted by the security forces continued. They encountered no interference from the Siamese government, who refused to accept any responsibility for the terrorists' presence and claimed that they sought sanctuary 'like gentlemen'.[1] The Malayan security forces were refused permission to enter the country to eliminate the terrorists who were planning to cross the border to attack targets in Malaya. In 1955, Chin assessed the advantages of increasing his cross-border attacks, and this assessment demonstrated the extent to which the supine policy of his host nation was placing their friendly neighbour at risk:

> Operating from sanctuary bases in southern Siam our guerillas could have staged fierce thrusts south across the border against government military outposts, police stations and other likely targets of opportunity. Each strike would be followed by a rapid withdrawal back to the relative safety of our sanctuaries ... The border was unquestionably long enough for us to have the choice of a wide variety of targets. Tactics of that nature tend to open up new opportunities ...[2]

The host nation seems to have attracted little criticism of its behaviour, and one wonders what their reaction would have been had the situation been reversed and large numbers of armed Siamese communist terrorists been allowed to set up 'sanctuary bases' south of the border in Malaya from which to carry out 'fierce thrusts' into Siam. The willing co-operation of the Siamese with the Japanese during the latter's wartime invasion of Malaya and Burma left their post-war reputation amongst their neighbours in tatters.

When I left Malaya in 1954, the number of terrorists being eliminated was averaging over 100 a month.[3] The British and Commonwealth infantry presence totalled twenty-two battalions, but the 6,000 remaining terrorists still had the support of the Min Yuen (some of whom were armed) and continued to dominate some 30,000 of the Aborigines in the hills.[4] Most importantly, of course, they still enjoyed the protection of the deep jungle. The resettlement of nearly all the Chinese squatters in New Villages had deprived the terrorists of much of their essential supplies, and this, coupled with the continued success of the security forces in killing them, led to a decline in terrorist morale and a surrender rate which rose from about 200 in 1954 to about 500 in 1958.[5]

By the end of 1955, Malaya was within twenty months of achieving independence from British rule, which was promised for 31 August 1957, and the communists knew that not only were they losing the armed struggle, but that independence would deprive them of their chief propaganda weapon, namely the claim that Malaya was suffering under colonial rule. Chin Peng thus proposed to the authorities that the two sides should negotiate to see if they could agree terms for an end to the fighting. At the discussions which were held at Baling in north Malaya in December 1955, the people of Malaya were represented by Tenku Abdul Rahman and Dato Sir Cheng Lock Tan, the leaders of their principal political party (the Alliance of Malays and non-communist Malayan Chinese) and the MCP was represented by Chin Peng and two colleagues. The Tenku offered amnesty terms and Chin demanded recognition of the MCP. Chin rejected the terms for an amnesty because they implied 'surrender' and thus loss of face, and the Tenku refused to recognise the MCP because, being under the control of China, it was not loyal to the Malayan people. Thus, the negotiations failed.[6]

Military operations against the terrorists continued, and their numbers steadily fell to about 600 in March 1960.[7] By the time the State of Emergency was officially ended on 31 July 1960, nearly all the surviving terrorists were lying low in Siam. The Emergency had lasted for twelve years, and had cost the lives of over 12,000 people, some 60 per cent of whom were terrorists.[8] Attempts by the armies of France and the USA to defeat communist guerillas in the jungles of Indo-China and Vietnam had failed disastrously, although the scale of the fighting there was vastly greater than it was in Malaya.

The defeat of the MRLA remains the only victory gained by the forces of democracy over a major insurgency by communist guerillas in the Far East.

An Assessment of Chin Peng

The 527 pages of Chin Peng's book, *My Side of History*, include detailed descriptions of his political beliefs and opinions, and the decisions he took as leader of the MCP, and they thus provide ample evidence with which to assess the man. Many of his opinions are flawed, and some of these are shown below, together with the page references to his book and my comments:

> At the end of the Second World War Britain resumed governing Malaya in order to exploit its resources and people to pay off her debts and maintain her Empire [p.9].

Britain's post-war debts resulted from the huge cost of fighting the Axis powers for longer than any of our allies did. When the war ended we were about to land in force in Malaya, to rescue its people from the Japanese occupiers. Did the debts that Britain incurred from fighting the Japanese in Burma, Ceylon, Hong Kong, India and Malaya not deserve to be repaid in part by those who ultimately benefited from our efforts?

By 1945 the British government had promised that every country in our Empire would be granted independence, as soon as they could show that they could effectively govern themselves. In July 1947 independence was granted to by far the largest part of our Empire, namely India and Pakistan. Similar grants were made to Burma in January 1948, and to Ceylon the following month. Thus, by the time Chin began the insurrection in June of that year, the majority of Britain's colonial empire (measured by population) had already been given independence, and the remaining colonies were on course to receive it. Independence for Malaya was specifically promised by the British Prime Minister on 13 April 1949.[9] In view of the grants of independence already made, and the promises of similar grants in future, the killing of innocent people in Malaya by Chin Peng's terrorists was totally unnecessary. Independence would no doubt have been granted before 1957, had there not been thousands of his men trying to impose a communist dictatorship on the country.

> Communism is 'infinitely fairer' than colonialism [p. 10].

Would anyone who knew of the treatment of the people in communist Russia during Stalin's regular purges, or in communist China during Mao's Cultural Revolution, or in communist Cambodia during Pol Pot's reign of terror, have thought that communism was infinitely fairer than colonialism?

Chin, who was living in China throughout the Cultural Revolution, regarded it as 'an important milestone in the evolution of world communism'.[10] Actually, 'an important gravestone' would have been a more accurate description of an event, the chief feature of which was the huge number of people killed. He must have observed plenty of examples of cruelty by the Red Guards and the Peoples' Liberation Army, so why did he think their behaviour was infinitely fairer than that of British colonialists?

Chin praises the London communist *Daily Worker* newspaper in 1952 for criticising the British government's policy in Malaya. Would any communist state have permitted a non-communist newspaper in their country to criticise its government's policy? In 1954, a conference of delegates from communist parties in the British Commonwealth was held in London.[11] Would any communist state have permitted conferences of non-communist parties to be held in its capital?

> The injustice of the British colonial legal process during the Emergency was demonstrated by the Lee Meng saga. [p. 350]

In 1952, a Chinese woman called Lee Meng was arrested and charged with carrying a grenade and consorting with terrorists, crimes which carried the death penalty. The prosecution witnesses at her trial were nine former terrorists. The accused denied being Lee Meng, or that she had ever carried a grenade. At the time those accused of terrorism were tried by two assessors from different races in Malaya, and a British judge. At her first trial, the two Asian assessors found her not guilty, but the British judge found her guilty and ordered a re-trial. At her second trial, the Asian assessor found her not guilty, but the British assessor and the British judge found her guilty, and she was sentenced to death. Various groups, including fifty British MPs, then petitioned the Sultan of Perak for clemency, and he commuted her sentence to life imprisonment. In 1964 she was released and exiled to China. Chin criticises the courts for hearing prosecution witnesses who owed their lives to the government, and for rejecting the not guilty verdicts of the three Asian assessors. At the time, Asian assessors who found terrorists guilty risked assassination by communist killer squads, which almost certainly explains their verdicts in the Lee Meng case. Asian assessors who found terrorists not guilty were, of course, never punished by the colonial authorities.

What were the facts? Chin Peng now admits that the accused really was Lee Meng (which proves she lied at her trial) and that she was his head courier, but he claims not to know whether she ever carried a weapon. This claim is absurd as he admits that she engaged in 'guerilla activities' while acting as his courier, and how many guerillas are not armed? As the prosecution witnesses were right in identifying her as Lee Meng, were they also not right in stating that she had been carrying a grenade?[12] All governments which encounter terrorism have to impose special judicial procedures to prevent the intimidation of jurors and witnesses.

> Chin now thinks that his announced aim should have been to establish 'independence for all political persuasions and all races' [p.238].

Such an announcement would have deliberately misled the public about the MCP's real intentions. How many communist states have allowed independence to people whose political beliefs differed from their own? In 1950 the MCP demonstrated how it dealt with anyone who held different political views. Their Malacca state secretary, a man with a distinguished wartime record with the MPAJA, wrote a booklet disagreeing with party policy regarding the distribution of land. He and his wife were executed.[13]

Even the few Malays who joined the communist insurgents were treated by the MCP far less well than their Chinese comrades. The Malays were rarely informed about policy matters. They were issued with obsolete firearms and poor-quality ammunition and food, and were not allowed to enter Chinese camps without permission, while the Chinese could freely enter Malay camps.[14] Did this not presage the treatment the Malay population would have received had the communists won?

> The British belief that the communist movement in Malaya was not a genuine nationalist movement is 'baseless' [p.357].

More than 90 per cent of the MCP membership consisted of ethnic Chinese, many of whom had been born in China or Siam and thus owed little allegiance to the Malay nation. The party's membership included hardly any from the Malay and Indian communities, which together formed nearly 60 per cent of the population of Malaya, so how can Chin claim that his party was a genuine nationalist movement?

The MCP had a branch in Peking and operated under the control of the Communist Party of China, which supplied advice, training, medical help, cash, a radio link between Peking and the MCP terrorists in Siam, and facilities for broadcasting propaganda throughout the Far East.[15] In 1955 Chin received a document jointly written by the communist parties of the Soviet Union and China, 'suggesting' that he should stop the armed struggle and instead concentrate on political matters. A month later, at the Baling negotiations, he tried to end the armed struggle and concentrate on his political aims. Following the Sino/Soviet split, he was 'urged' by the Chinese in 1961 to resume military operations and was promised the necessary funds to finance this. He immediately began making plans to do so. In view of this evidence, his rejection of claims that the MCP was under the control of the leading international communist states, is ridiculous.[16] The MCP was dedicated to promoting international communism, not Malay nationalism.

> The armed forces of the MCP 'did not eliminate a lot of innocent people' [p.105].

Official government statistics show that 2,473 civilians were murdered during the Emergency, and that 810 were abducted.[17] These figures have not been disputed by Chin. As nearly all those abducted had been taken into the jungle and murdered, the total number of 'innocent people' killed was at least 3,000. Was this not 'a lot'?

> The British were wrong to call MCP members 'communist terrorists' [p.105].

Nearly all members of the MCP's armed forces were communists, and people who deliberately kill innocent civilians are rightly called 'terrorists', so 'communist terrorists' was an absolutely accurate description of these men. In October 1951, more than three years after the Emergency had begun, Chin ordered his armed forces to cease 'acts of wanton terrorism', which confirms that he knew that those he was commanding were 'communist terrorists'.[18]

> He 'forced the British to the bargaining table long before they were prepared to sit there' [p. 10].

This is nonsense as the two men who represented the Malayan people at the first negotiations with Chin in 1955 were not British, but were a Malay and a Chinese who jointly led the Alliance Party which had been democratically elected and was preparing for independence, which would be granted two years later. During the negotiations Chin admitted that the Alliance negotiators 'were not the spokesmen of the British government and are not the running dog of the British government, the stooge of the British government.'[19] The Malay and Chinese negotiators had not been 'forced to the bargaining table', but had willingly gone there in the hope of persuading the MCP to end its campaign of terrorism and thus achieve peace for their country as soon as possible.

> During the Emergency 'between four and five thousand of my comrades were killed' [p.3].

The official government figure of the number of terrorists killed during the Emergency (excluding those who died of wounds) is 6,697.[20] This figure resulted mainly from a count of the number of corpses brought in to police stations by the security forces. Some terrorist corpses were never found and these, together with those who died of their wounds or sickness, would have increased the total. To be deducted from the total should be perhaps 100 innocent peasants who had been mistakenly assumed by the security forces to have been terrorists, and shot as a result.[21] Chin admits that he never had accurate figures of the number in the MRLA at any one time, and this explains his underestimate of the extent of their losses.[22]

> The British rather conveniently fail to provide statistics [of the number of terrorists hanged] [p.9].

Under the Emergency Regulations, all captured armed terrorists were liable to be executed after trial, but of the 1,296 captured, only 226 (or less than 18 per cent) were actually put to death. Some of those hanged were guilty of particularly appalling crimes, such as murdering children. These statistics were published in 1975 by the British author Anthony Short in his definitive account of the Emergency which was available to Chin and his co-authors.[23]

In addition to Chin's erroneous claims, his silence about certain subjects reveals his desire to conceal some embarrassing matters. The financing of the MCP, for example, was crucial to the terrorist campaign, but Chin tells us little about this subject, and a number of questions remain unanswered:

How much money did they receive from their Malayan Chinese supporters?
How much did they receive from the Peoples' Republic of China?
How much 'protection money' did they receive from the management of Malayan estates and mines?
What other organisations or individuals supplied them with money?
On what was the money spent?

In 1989, when the MCP finally surrendered, Chin sold more than 2,000 of their weapons to the Thai government, but he does not reveal how much he got for them or on what the proceeds were spent.

Chin's virulent attacks on British colonialism call for an explanation of why independence was not granted to Malaya until 1957. In the immediate post-war years, the country faced four major problems which prevented Britain from immediately granting independence, and made Malaya's political leaders reluctant to demand it at the time.[24] These problems were:

1 The extreme racial and religious division within the inhabitants of the country, with Malays and Chinese having populations of roughly equal size.
2 The antagonism which existed between the two races, with the Malays supplying virtually all the personnel of the native armed forces and the

Chinese controlling the majority of the native-owned economic wealth. The massacres of Muslims and Hindus, which had followed the grant of independence to India, made the British government wary of prematurely granting independence to colonies which had extreme racial and religious divisions. The Malay and Chinese leaders were also concerned that independence might result in conflict between their two races.

3 The lack of political and administrative experience of the leaders of each race.

4 The presence of thousands of armed terrorists dedicated to imposing communist rule on the country, irrespective of the views of the people.

No government could do anything about the first problem because, unlike in the Indian sub-continent, partition was not feasible as the Malays and Chinese were geographically too inter-mixed, and the country was too small to be divided into viable economic portions.

The only measure which the British could take to try to alleviate the second problem was to form a Federation Regiment to try to persuade non-Malays to join the Army, though unfortunately it failed to attract many Chinese recruits. After independence, the country's government introduced a number of measures which encouraged Malays to join the Chinese in acquiring wealth through involvement in business and industrial activities, and from training for academic and professional qualifications.

The third problem was solved by the setting up of political parties by the two main races and by the creation, in 1952, of local government councils with elected members. In 1946 the Malays set up the United Malays National Organisation, and in 1949 the non-communist Chinese set up the Malayan Chinese Association. By 1953 these parties were co-operating in local government elections, and became known as the Alliance Party. This co-operation, and the local councils, provided political and administrative experience for the leaders of the people and prepared them for greater responsibilities. By 1955 a Malayan government was established, following countrywide elections, with Tenku Abdul Rahman as the Chief Minister.

In 1954 the Colonial Secretary had announced that independence would be granted once the Emergency had been brought to a successful conclusion, but it took until 1957 for the security forces to virtually eliminate the terrorists from Malaya, and allow independence to be granted to a country no longer under an immediate threat of a communist take-over.[25]

In view of the colonial government's policy about the post-war problems outlined above, it can fairly be claimed that Britain did everything in its power to prepare Malaya for independence and democracy, and that the independent country, unlike a number of our other ex-colonies, has subsequently proved to be a great success.

It is now time to pass judgement on Chin Peng. For more than forty years he led a communist party which was dedicated to using terrorism to try to overthrow British colonial rule, and then to try to overthrow the democratically elected government of independent Malaysia. During the course of this long campaign, thousands of people were killed, and the races which suffered included Aborigines, African, Australian, British, Chinese, Fijian, Gurkha, Indian, Japanese, Malay and New Zealand. The cost of trying to end the Emergency, much of which fell on post-war Britain which could ill afford to finance it, was huge. Halfway through the Emergency, the British armed forces in Malaya were costing Britain £550 million per annum.[26] Sabotage of estates, mines and transport, and the murder of managers and workers, set back the economy. The communist campaign failed, and all the human suffering was in vain. If ever a leader was guilty of presiding over crimes against humanity it is Chin Peng, and he should have been tried for this offence. He can be admired for his determination and courage in the face of endless difficulties and dangers, but his dedication to terrorism is unforgivable. Although world communism has suffered enormous setbacks in recent years, the determination and ruthlessness of men like Chin Peng make it a continuing risk to democratic countries.

Notes

1 Short, p.487.
2 Chin Peng, pp.393-94.
3 See the table on p.136
4 Postgate, p.160; Short, p.441.
5 Miller, *Menace*, p.219; Short, pp.507-08.
6 Short, pp.460-71.
7 Ibid., p.493.
8 Ibid., pp.507-08,together with estimates made by the present author of the number of wounded terrorists who died of their wounds (25 per cent) and the number of missing civilians murdered by terrorists (75 per cent).
9 Short, p.327.
10 Chin Peng, p.446.
11 Ibid., pp.302, 351.
12 Ibid., pp.338-50.
13 Ibid., pp.256-57.
14 A. Chin, pp.39-40.
15 Ibid., p.64.
16 Chin Peng, pp.367, 403-04, 429, 433.
17 Short, pp.507-08.
18 Chin Peng, p.315.
19 Ibid., p.377.

20 Short, pp.507–08.

21 Barber, p.97.

22 Chin Peng, p.398.

23 Short, pp.384, 507–08. Short was employed by the University of Malaysia in 1960, when it agreed with the government of Malaysia that he should write the official history of the Emergency. He was given full access to the Malaysian government's secret papers, though access to the British government's equivalent records was denied. He presented his manuscript to the Malaysian government in 1968, but three years later he was told they would not publish it, probably because they thought it was too revealing. Fortunately, he found a commercial publisher in 1975; Short, p.1.

24 Ibid., p.504.

25 Ibid., p.13.

26 Ibid., p.348.

EPILOGUE

Many events in life have later consequences, some humorous, some surprising, some tragic. Like Spencer Chapman, I did not find my first few months after demobilisation particularly easy.[1] My first job was with an international oil company in London, and some unwelcome memories soon resurfaced. While walking down Oxford Street one lunchtime, a terrorist fired at me which caused me to dive behind the bushes. As I raised my carbine to shoot him, I saw that he was a backfiring car, that my carbine was my umbrella, and that the bushes were planted in tubs outside the entrance to Selfridges. My work included calculating the profitability of the company's sales of aviation gasolene, which reminded me of the stinking latrines I had blown up with this product at Triang, and the fury of the visiting general whose helicopter could not be re-fuelled. After life in the Army, I found that sitting in front of a calculating machine all day long was excruciatingly boring. The behaviour of the Departmental Manager reminded me very much of that of Major Rosslyn, and as my civilian boss was most unlikely to move to another company like Rosslyn had done, I soon made that move myself.

While I was working for another company in London, I interviewed an applicant for a sales post who, when I read his file, turned out to be the gunnery officer who had commanded the battery which had wounded my English subaltern friend in the bottom. He did not recognise me, and I was unable to resist teasing him about the inaccuracy of his firing that day in December 1953. He was astounded that I knew anything about the incident, but later was delighted when I told him I would recommend him for the post. Unfortunately, he did not perform well and soon left.

Shortly afterwards, a Colonel in my English regiment contacted me to ask why I had not joined their Territorial Army battalion. I explained that the icy reception I had received at the regimental depot in 1953 had convinced me that peacetime service in the regiment was not for me. He was very understanding, and invited me to lunch at his London club where he explained that at the time of my visit the depot had been largely staffed by officers who had been sent home from Korea for incompetence. The Territorials, he said, were a much better bunch whose company I would enjoy. I duly joined for a few years, but did not find peacetime soldiering exciting. Until 1957 National Servicemen were obliged to join the TA for three and a half years after demobilisation, but many ignored this rule and escaped punishment. A full complement for an infantry battalion was around twenty-five officers and 600 men, but the extent of the widespread refusal to join the TA became apparent when I attended my TA battalion's summer camp at Castlemartin in Pembrokeshire, and found that our party consisted of eighteen officers, but only seventeen other ranks.

A sad incident occurred on our last night at Castlemartin. We held a dinner in the mess to mark the end of the camp, and afterwards everyone had to give a solo performance. My contribution was a recitation of the first dozen or so verses of 'The Ball of Kirremuir', which I had memorised long before for use on such occasions, and others recited similar obscene poems such as 'Eskimo Nell'. By far the most entertaining performance, however, was delivered by our mess treasurer, an ancient retired officer with First World War ribbons on his chest. In a quavering voice, he sang a ditty about Edwardian bathing belles on Brighton Beach. All the words were polite, but all the phrases were double entendre, and conveyed clear pictures of what was going on inside the bathing machines which were drawn up on the beach while the young ladies inside were entertaining young gentlemen. We vowed to bring a tape recorder to the next mess night to preserve this unique ditty for posterity, but alas we were not to have the opportunity, as in the early hours of the following morning the singer blew out his brains with a revolver. A subsequent investigation revealed a shortfall of a few hundred pounds in the mess funds. If he had confessed to the Colonel, a whip round would have been organised among the officers to replace the missing money, but the shame was too much for him to bear.

A number of later parties in Somerset produced some amusing incidents. I received a crushing put-down from the wife of a retired Colonel when she asked if I had ever been in the Army. I told her that during National Service I had been commissioned into a county infantry regiment and seconded to the Malay Regiment. 'Ah,' she said pityingly, 'A conscript in the native infantry'. This description (which I was tempted to use as the title for this book) is, of course, strictly accurate, but though 'conscript' sounds derogatory, it should be remembered that in the days of National Service one could not become a 'volunteer' unless one wanted a long-term career in the Army. The term 'native infantry' is also disparaging, but it could be applied to regiments like the Gurkhas, many of whose officers later became generals, and four became field-marshals.[2] Having transferred out of a service corps into an infantry regiment, I felt somewhat hurt by her description, but when next we met I regained a little respect when I let drop the fact that I was an Old Eatonian. This is the title used by members of the Eaton Hall Officer Cadet School Reunion Association, and fortunately I was not asked to spell the word after 'Old'. Alternatively, I could equally accurately have told her that I had been at school at Harrow, which would have earned similar respect provided I was not asked whether the words 'County Grammar School' should have followed the name of the town. When she asked what my Cornish surname meant in English, I told her 'Newhouse' ('chy', house, 'noweth', new), but resisted the temptation to reveal that the latin equivalent which occurs in some early manuscripts is 'Casanova' ('casa', house, 'nova', new).

At another party I met a slim, grey-haired lady, who mentioned that her husband had been in the Malay Regiment in the 1950s. I asked which battalion, and she said, 'The sixth'. I began to tell her about my first conversation with Colonel Skinny, and had got as far as the threat of a court martial and was about to continue with the bit about the adjutant's wife, when something made me ask, 'What post did your husband hold?' 'He was the adjutant,' she replied. When I'd recovered, I asked if he was at the party. 'No,' she said. 'He went down the road long ago'. I have often wondered how many young officers of her acquaintance had gone down the road long ago on their way to join a parachute course in Singapore.

In 1992 I was surprised to read a statement about the Malay Regiment in a book of reminiscences written by a retired Brigadier. He described what British regiments did with officers who, for various reasons, were regarded as being unsuitable. It was not always easy to find postings for these men, but:

> Once upon a time this was a simple matter. They were sent to the Malay Regiment, who habitually shot their officers every six months or so, which solved the problem.

He does not appear to have been joking, but he cites no source for his statement. While I was with the regiment I never heard that any officer had ever been shot accidentally or deliberately by his men. Although I disbelieve his claim, I am glad his book was not available for me to read while I was on my way to Malaya![3]

A tragic consequence of wartime life in Malaya was the deaths of Pat Noone and Spencer Chapman. Both men had several interests in common. Noone was an anthropologist and Chapman wished he had become one.[4] Before the war both had enjoyed lovers from races not usually chosen by English Oxbridge graduates – Noone had acquired an Aboriginal girl, and Chapman, an Eskimo. Both men had spent years in the Malayan jungle. In 1934, while Noone was returning to Singapore by boat after leave in England, he became engaged to an English girl, but the relationship soon ended and she became engaged to a man called Goode. This episode was welcomed by the ex-pats in Singapore with shouts of 'Good afternoon!' Later that year, Noone 'married' his Aboriginal mistress, who was an attractive young girl called Anjang from the Temiar tribe, and employed a young Temiar brave called Uda to act as his guide during his jungle treks. Temiar custom permitted younger brothers to sleep with the wives of their elder brothers in the absence of the latter, and as Noone had foolishly told Anjang that he regarded Uda as his younger brother she slept with the young man whenever Noone was away.

After the Japanese invaded in 1941, Noone stayed in the jungle and spent some time with the MPAJA, acting as liaison officer between them and the Aborigines. He never emerged from the jungle at the end of the war, and great efforts were made to find out what had happened to him, but the Aborigines denied all knowledge of his whereabouts, and the members of the MPAJA also appeared to know nothing. In 1950 Anjang emerged from the jungle, but she was ill and soon died without revealing anything about Noone. In the spring of 1954 a group of Aborigines who had been helping the terrorists surrendered to the authorities, and their leader told Noone's younger brother Richard, who was then Head of the Department of Aborigines, that late in 1943 Noone had been murdered by Uda, who had blowpiped him at the Sungei Wi River near the Cameron Highlands, and had finished him off with a parang. Noone was buried at Kuala Wi, and his murder was made the subject of an Aboriginal taboo, which explains why it took so long for the truth to emerge. After Noone's death, Anjang lived with Uda, but it is not known what happened to him after she died. The lives of the Temiar had always been dominated by dreams, and Uda had said that he had dreamt that Noone intended to take Anjang away from her people, and make the Temiar fight the Japanese, which would have led to many tribal deaths. To western minds Uda's lust for Anjang seems to be the more likely cause of the murder of Noone.

The general public did not hear about Noone's death until 1958 when Dennis Holman published a book called *Noone of the Ulu*, so when I was in Malaya I was one of the many who wanted to find out what had happened to him. When on my last operation in 1954 I came across an unusual grave I wondered whether it might be Noone's, but four years later it emerged that he had been buried a long way away from the grave I had found.[5]

Despite the official recognition of Spencer Chapman's wartime services (promotion to Lieutenant-Colonel, and the award of the DSO and bar), and the great success of his book *The Jungle is Neutral* (even Chin Peng carried a copy with him in the jungle), he felt he never subsequently achieved all that his talents deserved.[6] In his foreword to Chapman's book, Field Marshal Earl Wavell compared his feats of endurance with those of Lawrence of Arabia in the First World War, but added that, 'Chapman has never received the publicity or fame that were his predecessor's lot.'[7] After he left the Army, Chapman was unable to settle for long in any job, and his last post was that of warden of a hall at the University of Reading.

For years he had suffered from medical problems, and as he approached the retirement age of sixty-five he became increasingly worried, both about his health and his financial position. He applied to the university for an extension of his appointment, but in 1971 his request was turned down and he committed suicide. A post-mortem revealed no hidden illness (which makes the reason for his medical problems something of a mystery) and there seems to have been no real reason for his financial worries, so it is difficult to decide why he chose to take his life.[8] Perhaps he was embittered at never achieving the success he felt he deserved, and was unwilling to face a future marred by sickness and depression.

A few years after his death I paid a nostalgic visit to Malaya and, when I spent a night in the jungle on the bank of the Sungei Mengkuang River near Triang in Pahang, I hoped to meet his ghost and that of Pat Noone. It seemed to me to be a perfect place for such manifestations, as it had associations with the three of us. Chapman had camped there in 1942, as I had done in 1954 when I had found a grave nearby which I thought might be Noone's.

The camp-site was like a dark green room as the clearing was roofed by the canopy of trees, and walled by curtains of creepers. As evening drew on, the fading light gave way to the pale green glow of the luminous leaves which carpeted the ground, and the fireflies which floated just above. I sat on a log with a bottle of scotch, a jug of water and two spare glasses at my feet, awaiting the arrival of my guests, and listening to the noises which heralded the onset of night and echoed the sounds of the past. Was that scream from the river bank Noone's last shriek as he was hacked to death by Uda's parang? Was that sigh from the creepers Chapman's last breath before he pulled the trigger of his shotgun? Alas, neither man's ghost came to tell me about their lives or deaths, and my long solitary wait left me depressed. Like Chapman, I began to question whether I had done enough with my life. Like Noone, I thought that perhaps I had done too much of the wrong thing. When will I join them, I wondered, and where will it be? Do we have souls destined to meet in Valhalla, or merely bodies destined to rot into oblivion?

Notes

1 Barker, p.239.
2 Farwell, p.124.
3 Starling, pp.100-101.
4 Spencer Chapman, *Living*, p.164.

5 Holman, pp.28, 55-56, 112, 138, 175-76, 209-11; Noone, pp.144-195.

6 Miller, *Jungle*, p.124.

7 Spencer Chapman, *The Jungle*, pp.v-vii.

8 Barker, p.362 and footnote.

Bibliography of Books Cited in the Text

All were published in London, unless otherwise stated.

Allen, L., Burma, *The Longest War 1941–45*, 1998 edition.
Animal Life, The New Larousse Encyclopedia of, 1980.
Annual Abstract of Statistics, 2004.
Atom, The Conduct of Anti-Terrorist Operations in Malaya, H.Q. Malaya, 1952.
Barber, N., *The War of the Running Dogs*, 1971.
Barker, R., *One Man's Jungle*, 1975.
Baynes, J., *Urquhart of Arnhem*, 1993.
Bose, M., Raj, *Secrets, Revolution. A Life of Subhas Chandra Bose*, 2004.
Brown, M., *The Imperial War Museum Book of the Western Front*, 1993.
Campbell, A., *Jungle Green*, 1953.
Carew, T., *How the Regiments got their Nicknames*, 1974.
Chin, A., *The Communist Party of Malaya*, Kuala Lumpur, 1994.
Churchill, W.S., *The Second World War*, 1951.
Cloake, J., *Templer, Tiger of Malaya*, 1985.
Cooper, Duff, *Old Men Forget*, 1953.
Crockett, A., *Green Beret, Red Star*, 1954.
Delano, A, *Warriors of Zion, BBC History*, Vol.6, No.3, March 2005.
The Dictionary of National Biography, Vol.24, Oxford, 2004.
Farwell, B., *The Gurkhas*, 1984.
Follows, R., *The Jungle Beat*, 1990.
Gaylor, J., *Military Badge Collecting*, 1996.
Gullick, J.M., *Malaya*, 1963.
Holman, D., *Noone of the Ulu*, 1958.
Ibrahim bin Ismail, General Tan Sri, *Have you met Mariam?*, Johor Bahru, 1984.
Jackson, P., *Endangered Species: Tigers*, 1990.

Keegan, J., *The Second World War*, 1989.
Kennedy, J., *A History of Malaya*, 1962.
Kirby, S. Woodburn, *The War Against Japan*, Vol. 1, 1957.
Singapore: The Chain of Disaster, 1971.
Lunt, J., *Imperial Sunset*, 1981.
Mains, T., *Sandhurst to the Khyber 1932–1940*, Durham, 1999.
Middlebrook, M., *The First Day of the Somme*, 1971.
Middlebrook, M. and Mahoney, P., *Battleship*, Harmondsworth, 1979.
Miers, R., *Shoot to Kill*, 1959.
Miller, H., *Menace in Malaya*, 1954.
Jungle War in Malaya, 1972.
Neillands, R., *A Fighting Retreat*, 1996.
The Great War Generals, 1999.
Newman, O., and Foster, A,. *The Value of the Pound 1900–1993*, 1995.
Niven, D., *The Moon's a Balloon*, Penguin edition of 1994.
Noone, R., *Rape of the Dream People*, 1972.
O'Ballance, E., *Malaya: The Communist Insurgent War, 1948–1960.*
Orchard, L. B., First World War Diary copied by Mary Toomey, 1999.
Postgate, M., *Operation Firedog: Air Support in the Malayan Emergency*, HMSO, 1992.
Peng, Chin, *My Side of History*, Singapore, 2003.
Putkowski, J. and Sykes, J., *Shot at Dawn*, 1992.
The Review, Quarterly Journal of the Naval Collectors and Research Association.
Robinson, J.B. Perry, *Transformation in Malaya*, 1956.
Royle, T., *The Best Years of Their Lives*, 1986.
Scurr, J., *Jungle Campaign*, Lewes, 1998.
Sheppard, M.C. ff., *The Malay Regiment 1933–1947*, Kuala Lumpur, 1947.
Short, A., *The Communist Insurrection in Malaya 1948–1960*, 1975.
Spencer Chapman, F., *The Jungle is Neutral*, The Reprint Society, 1950.
Living Dangerously, 1953.
Starling, J., *Soldier On!* Tunbridge Wells, 1992.
Sutton, D.J., ed., *The Story of the Royal Army Service Corps*, 1983.
Terraine, J., *The Smoke and the Fire*, 1980.
Thompson, J., *Victory in Europe*, 1994.
Thompson, R., *Defeating Communist Insurgency*, 1966.
Toye, H., *The Springing Tiger*, 1959.
van Emden, R. and Humphries, S., *Veterans: The Last Survivors of the Great War*, 1998.
Ziegler, P., *Mountbatten: The Official Biography*, 1985.

Appendix: Air-Dropped Leaflets

In 1953 more than 90 million Government leaflets were air dropped into the jungle to try to persuade more terrorists to surrender.[1] Because they could not read Chinese my parents did not keep the examples I sent home, so I had none available for the first edition of this book. After Mr Mervyn Selway of North Petherton had read it, however, he kindly contacted me, and allowed me to photocopy the leaflets which he had collected while serving in the Somerset Light Infantry in Malaya in 1953 and 1954. I then had them translated into English. The leaflets varied in content and presentation, and I have chosen six to illustrate some of the differences:

1 An impressive looking safe conduct pass in five languages signed by General Templer.
2 A cartoon advising terrorists what action they should take to surrender.
3 A picture of a senior terrorist leader decapitated by his bodyguards who then surrendered.
4 A cartoon with criticisms of senior terrorist leaders.
5 A cartoon illustrating what features terrorist leaders wanted in their men.
6 Pictures of six male and six female surrendered terrorists who appear well fed and cheerful.

It is impossible to estimate how effective the numerous leaflets were in encouraging surrenders. General Templer's safe conduct pass promised good treatment, food, cigarettes, medical attention if required, and $500 rewards for those helping terrorists to surrender. The leaflets almost certainly caused many terrorists to seriously consider giving up, but some were afraid they would be shot by their comrades or the Security Forces while trying to do so, and some were suspicious about what their treatment would be like after surrendering. The terrorist leaders warned their men that those who surrendered would be tortured by the Security Forces, and in his safe conduct pass Templer referred to this warning and advised worried terrorists to consult local people about this. The terrorist leaders punished those they caught with leaflets in their possession.

Note:
[1]O' Ballance, p.131 f.1.

Example 1: Safe conduct pass, translation of Chinese wording

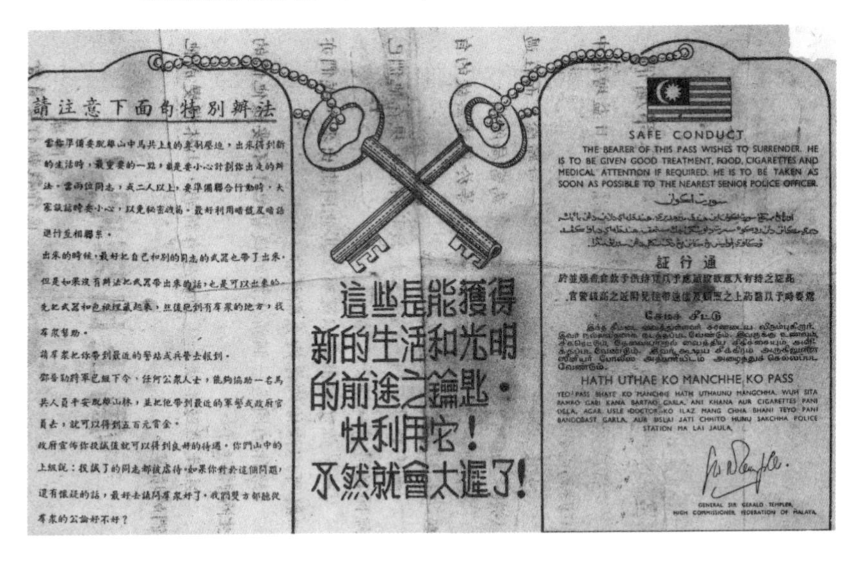

Panel beneath keys:

These are the keys to a new life and a bright future.
Take hold of them before it is too late!

Panel on left:

Pay attention to these six special instructions:

When you are prepared to disengage from the rule of your communist superiors and come out to get your new life, the most important thing is to plan your escape very carefully. When two or more comrades are discussing the escape plan they should be very careful with their conversation, not to let anyone know. Ideally, use some code.

When you come out it is better to bring out your weapon and those of your comrades. However, if this is not possible, it is still all right.

Bury your weapons and packets and go to where you can find local residents for help. Ask local people to take you to the nearest Police Station or Military Camp.

General Templer has ordered that anyone who helps a Malayan communist escape from the jungle safely and takes them to the nearest Police Officer or Government Officials will be rewarded by $500 cash.

You will receive [medical] treatment once the Government accepts your surrender. Your superiors must have told you that your comrades were tortured after surrendering. On this point, if you have any suspicions you had better ask the local people. Let us both listen to them. Wouldn't that be good?

Example 2: Strip cartoon advising terrorists how they should surrender

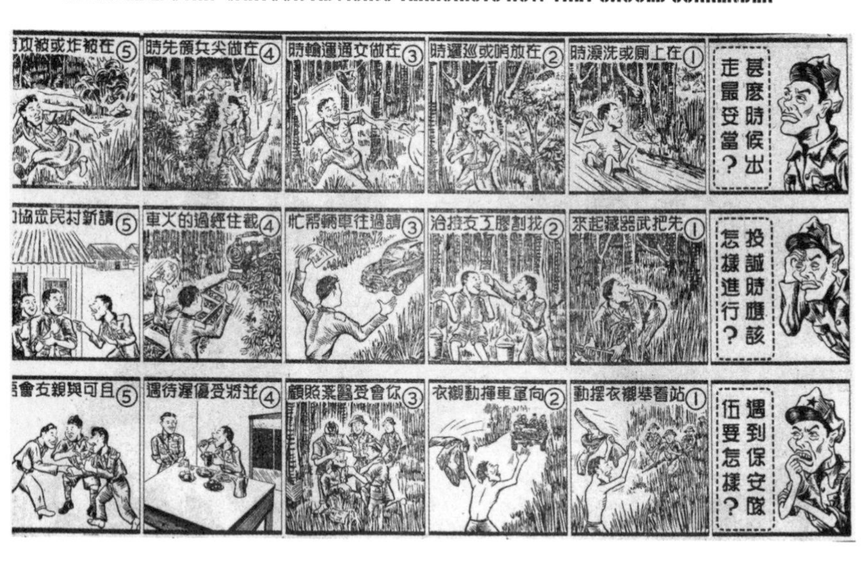

Top strip reading right to left:

What is the best time to come out?

1 When going to the toilet or having a bath

2 When at post or patrolling

3 When moving from one place to another

4 When at the front of a patrol

5 When being bombed or attacked

Middle strip reading right to left:

What to do to surrender?

1 First hide your weapons

2 Make contact with rubber plantation workers

3 Ask for help from passing vehicles
4 Stop a train
5 Ask residents for help

Bottom strip reading right to left:
How to react when meeting a patrol?
1 Stand still and wave your shirt
2 Wave your shirt to military vehicles
3 Receive medical treatment
4 Receive hospitality
5 Reach friends, family and relatives

All this advice seems sensible, although a uniformed terrorist meeting a patrol would be liable to be shot by the leading scout before he could take off his shirt to wave. In the first few seconds of such encounters the scout would probably not realise that the terrorist was unarmed.

EXAMPLE 3: A PICTURE OF A CENTRAL COMMITTEE REPRESENTATIVE COMRADE 'SHORTY' AH KOEK WHOSE HEAD WAS 'LIBERATED' BY HIS OWN COMRADES

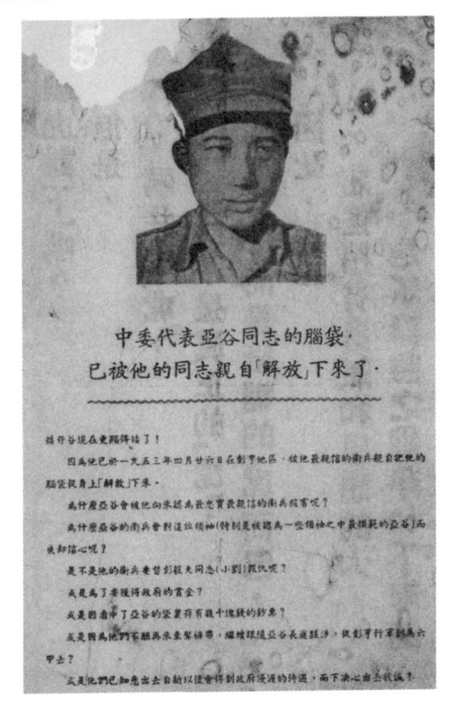

'Shorty' Koek is now shorter! [He was 4ft 9in.] Because his head was removed by his own most trusted guards on 26 April 1953. [The bodyguards then surrendered.]

Why was Ah Koek killed by the guards whom he thought were most loyal and trustworthy? Why did Ah Koek's own guards lose confidence in this great leader, especially the one thought to be of all leaders?

Was it that his guards wanted revenge for [the execution?] of Comrade Peng Yifu?

Or reward from the Government?

Or they liked the couple of thousand dollars in his pocket?

Or because they didn't want to tighten their belts and continue the long painful march with Ah Koek to Malacca?

Or they already knew that they will be well treated by the Government after surrender, and so decided to come out of the jungle?

Example 4: A cartoon illustrating 'the qualifications of a superior officer'

上級領袖的資格:

1. 大眼睛:能够監視下級同志們的一切行動.
2. 小耳朵:所以聽不見下級同志們的抗議.
3. 大嘴巴:用以整天發號施令,講自由平等的騙話,和狼吞虎嚥,大食大喝.
4. 小胸膛:縮小目標,避免鎗弹射畫.
5. 大肚子:以備容納珍貴的補品和好的食品.
6. 纖纖小手:便於解開束腰帶.
7. 大屁股:因爲同志們整天忙着辛苦去運粮和收捐,他却終日閒坐着.

1. Big eyes: to monitor every movement of his subordinate comrades.
2. Small ears: to ignore disagreements and criticisms from subordinate comrades.
3. Big mouth: to give orders all day and night, and issue lies about freedom and equality and eat and drink a lot.
4. Small chest: to be a small target for bullets.
5. Big stomach: to hold precious food and provisions.
6. Small tender hands: to loosen his belt.
7. Big bum: sits all day while comrades are busy moving stores and collecting taxes.

EXAMPLE 5: A CARTOON ILLUSTRATING THE 'QUALIFICATIONS OF A MODEL SOLDIER'

1. Blind eyes: so that he does not see the mistakes and bad habits of his superiors.
2. Big ears: so that he can be loaded with a hail of lies and unreasonable orders from his superiors.
3. No mouth: so that he cannot talk behind his boss's back and does not need to eat.
4. Big chest: so that he can block the bullets from his superiors behind him.

5. Small stomach: so that he saves food and solves the food shortage.
6. Rough hands: so that he can do dirty and heavy work.
7. Big feet: so that he can walk through swamp and jungle.

In fact the last two features are desirable qualifications for the Security Force troops as well as terrorists!

Example 6: Pictures of six male and female surrendered terrorists who appear to be well-fed and cheerful

They have already started a new life. Why don't you want to be a new person?